THE
ALIAS

MANDI TUCKER SLACK

BONNEVILLE BOOKS
SPRINGVILLE, UTAH

ISBN 13: 978-1-59955-509-6

Published by Bonneville Books, an imprint of Cedar Fort, Inc., 2373 W. 700 S., Springville, UT 84663

Distributed by Cedar Fort, Inc., www.cedarfort.com

LIBRARY OF CONGRESS CATALOGING-IN-PUBLICATION DATA

Slack, Mandi (Mandi Jean), 1980- author.
  The alias / Mandi Slack.
    p. cm.
  Summary: Recently divorced Jacey Grayson is questioned by the FBI about her ex-husband who is involved in drug trafficking and murder. Frightened, Jacey and her son hide among rural Mormons in a small town in Utah. Afraid Jacey will help the FBI arrest him, her ex-husband finds them, kidnaps their son and attempts to kill his ex-wife.
  ISBN 978-1-59955-509-6
  1. Criminal investigation--Fiction. I. Title.

  PS3619.L328 A93
  813'.6--dc22

                    2010045404

Cover design by Megan Whittier
Cover design © 2011 by Lyle Mortimer
Edited and typeset by Heidi Doxey

Printed in the United States of America

10 9 8 7 6 5 4 3 2 1

Printed on acid-free paper

For my loving parents, Scott and Brenda, who have always encouraged my dreams, loved so unselfishly, and lifted my spirits through all of life's ups and downs. I love you both and treasure the moments we've shared.

Also, a huge thank you to my wonderful husband. Without your encouragement, all the extra diapers you've changed, and all the meals you've cooked, this book would have never been finished. Love you!

ONE

Jacey Grayson exhaled noisily as she gazed out at the heavy afternoon traffic. It was nearing three o'clock. She needed to finish up or she would be late again. Blaze hated when she was late. The café was unusually packed, and Jacey knew Ian would need her to stay, but she couldn't, not today. She desperately needed to spend some time with her son. She felt guilty that she had to spend so much time working.

Working as a full-time waitress was hard, demanding work, but she had been lucky to land a job at such a well-established café. And even though the work was long and difficult, the tips paid off, and Jacey felt good knowing that she was able to support herself and Blaze. In a few more months she would have enough saved so that they could finally have a place of their own.

The arrangement had worked out great in the beginning. Since the divorce, she and her son had been living with Melissa and Melissa's daughter, Jenny. Jacey and Blaze had finally found a place where she could feel relatively safe from John. Melissa was always willing to watch Blaze after school if Jacey had to work late, which happened too often, and Melissa had never given the impression that she wanted Jacey or Blaze gone. However, Jacey knew it was still an intrusion on Melissa and Jenny's lives. Once she had saved enough, she could move into one of the apartment complexes closer to Blaze's new school, and they would still be close to Melissa. Jacey hoped that maybe once they settled into an apartment and a life of their own, Blaze would feel more comfortable with their new situation.

The divorce had been hard on Blaze, and long before the divorce, he had become withdrawn and quiet. Jacey couldn't get him to open up. She knew the things that Blaze had seen when she and John fought had affected him, but she couldn't get him to talk about it very often. Maybe once they got on their own he would begin to change. Maybe he would smile again. Maybe they would *both* smile again.

"Table six's finished up, Jace."

Jacey turned from the window, pulled from her thoughts. "Great! Thanks, Mary. I'm so glad they're finally done. I've got to get out of here soon."

The older woman nodded understandingly. "That boy of yours is waiting?"

Jacey nodded quickly as she grabbed a large tray off the dish rack. "Yes, and I promised I'd be there on time today." She gave a short laugh. "We'll see."

"Well then, go on." Mary put a hand on Jacey's slim forearm. "Let me take this one. You go get that boy of yours. Summer school is bad enough. Don't make him wait any longer than he has to."

"Oh, I can't let you do that. Your tables are packed today."

"I think I can handle one extra clean-up. I'm not that old." Mary winked playfully as she took the tray from Jacey's hand.

Jacey sighed. "If you're sure. Thanks, Mary. I owe you one."

"Go on. Get out of here or you'll be late."

Jacey smiled gratefully before she rushed to her locker to retrieve her purse. She was thankful Ian wasn't around at the moment. Her boss didn't care for table swapping, but Jacey knew Mary never paid attention to Ian's gruff ways.

She stepped out into the hot July sun and made her way across the steaming black pavement. Her Jetta was parked several yards away, as Ian always preferred employees to park further from the café, leaving more parking up front for his diners.

Jacey breathed a sigh of relief when she reached her vehicle. She would be on time today. She fished around in her purse, trying to locate her keys just as a deep voice called out, "Jacey Trent."

Startled, Jacey turned to watch as two men approached her. Her heart hammered against her ribs when both men held out their badges for her to see.

"Mrs. Trent?"

"Yes?" Jacey acknowledged guardedly.

"I'm Special Agent Ronald, and this is my partner, Special Agent Parker," the older man proceeded. "We're with the FBI. We'd like to ask you a few questions regarding your husband, John Trent, and his association with a man named Rafael Vizcaino. Do you know him?"

Jacey stared, open-mouthed for a moment. *The FBI,* she thought numbly. *What's going on?*

"I know Rafael Vizcaino. What—what is this about?"

Had John found her? Jacey's hands trembled as she moved to brush a lock of hair off her damp forehead.

"What can you tell us about Rafael Vizcaino, Mrs. Trent?"

Confused, Jacey shook her head slightly. "I know he's John's best friend and business associate. John has known Rafael for years. They've worked very close through the years. He—well, he helped John open several of his restaurants in the Chicago area. John had him over for dinner many times to discuss business. That—well, that's about all I know."

Agent Ronald nodded and returned his badge to the inside of his expensive suit coat.

Agent Parker stepped closer. "So you know him pretty well then?" the younger agent asked. His blue eyes quickly ran the length of Jacey's apron-clad body, and she shifted uncomfortably.

"No. I just said I knew who he was," Jacey replied evenly.

"Hot today, isn't it?" Agent Ronald smiled, running a hand through his receding hair.

"Yes, it is," Jacey responded.

"Tell me, Mrs. Trent, are you aware of Vizcaino's illegal activities?" he asked.

Jacey could feel the blood rush from her cheeks. "What—what do you mean? I had no idea. What sort of illegal activities?"

"Drug trafficking, money laundering. We also believe he and

his operation are behind the disappearance of Gary Walbeck. I'm sure you've heard mention of it in the news."

Jacey searched her mind quickly. The name sounded vaguely familiar, and she nodded slowly. "He's the journalist for *The Tribune* that disappeared." Jacey said. "Why would Rafael be behind his disappearance?"

"Do you know Sharon Ivan?" Agent Parker jumped in.

"No." Jacey shook her head. "I don't believe so. I've never heard of her."

"Sharon Ivan is Vizcaino's defense attorney. Gary Walbeck has spent a lot of time investigating the Vizcaino's crime ring over the last year or so. His last interview was with Ms. Ivan. Yesterday Sharon Ivan's body was found in an abandoned warehouse. The body had been there a while."

Jacey swallowed hard, feeling slightly faint. "So," she began hesitantly, "you think Rafael is behind her murder? He's part of some crime ring?"

"Yes, he is, and yes, that is exactly what we think, Mrs. Trent. We believe he may have played a part in her murder."

Jacey nodded. "Okay." She felt breathless. "But—what do I have to do with all of this? He and John—I didn't really know Rafael all that well."

Agent Parker's blue eyes narrowed. His eyes skimmed across Jacey's pale face. "Aren't you aware that your husband—?"

"Ex-husband," Jacey cut in abruptly. "John and I are divorced."

"I see," Agent Parker acknowledged with a smirk. "Your *ex*-husband, then, is involved with the Vizcaino gang. We have reason to believe that Trent has been using his restaurants to aid Vizcaino's operations. He and Rafael Vizcaino have set up a fairly large money-laundering operation, and they've been importing drugs into the country through shipments to his restaurants and other businesses."

Jacey felt sick. How could John be involved in all of this?

"Were you aware of this?" Agent Ronald asked quietly.

"No," she admitted weakly. "John and I have been separated for awhile now. Our divorce was finalized about three months ago. I'm not sure what—"

"How long were you and John Trent married, Mrs. Trent?" Agent Parker cut in.

"It's Grayson. Jacey Grayson." Jacey lifted a shaking hand to her temple. It was so hot.

"Ms. Grayson—sorry. How long were you and John Trent married?" the agent repeated.

"Ms. Grayson, you look pale." Agent Ronald stepped forward, grasping Jacey by the arm. "Perhaps this has come as a shock. Why don't you sit down?" He led her to a nearby cement planter, and she gratefully sat down on its sunbaked edge.

"John and I were married for eight years," she told the agents faintly.

"And during your eight-year marriage to John Trent, you never had any suspicions of Vizcaino and John's associations? Trent's restaurant chain suddenly boomed about the same time he met Vizcaino. You were never curious about that?"

Jacey's eyes narrowed. What were these men trying to imply? She felt sick with shock. "No, I never really—John and I never discussed work. He never felt a need to include me in his business affairs." Jacey's heart thumped as the agents eyed one another.

Agent Ronald cleared his throat. "And you've never met Sharon Ivan?"

"No. Why?" she asked suspiciously.

"Your husband knew her, very well in fact. Over the last year, they've been seen together quite often."

Jacey swallowed hard. John had been having another affair. It shouldn't bother her now, but it did. It hurt every time, despite her and John's problems. Jacey sighed. "What are you trying to say, Agent Ronald?"

Agent Ronald glanced knowingly at Agent Parker, and he asked again, "So, you've never met or heard of Sharon Ivan?"

Jacey's heart beat fast. She had done nothing, yet they were interrogating her as if she were a criminal. "I told you *no*," she replied. Her voice rose in pitch. "Look, if you're suggesting John had an affair with this—this woman, you're probably correct. John had several affairs during the years we were married, but I do not know, nor have I ever met, Sharon Ivan."

"She's dead, Ms. Grayson," Agent Parker reminded her coldly.

Jacey's face turned white. Did they suspect her of killing Sharon Ivan? This couldn't be happening to her.

Noting Jacey's reaction, Agent Ronald spoke calmly, "Do you believe that John Trent may have had anything to do with Sharon Ivan's death, Ms. Grayson?"

"You think John killed her?" Jacey's eyes broadened.

"We don't know that, but we do suspect he may have. Ms. Ivan was the Vizcaino's defense attorney, and we have very probable evidence that John Trent was having an affair with Ms. Ivan. Your husband is operating with the Vizcaino crime organization. Gary Walbeck's last interview was with Ms. Ivan. All this combined leads us to believe she may have posed a possible threat to their operation. She may have known too much or she may have revealed too much to Walbeck. What we know is we have one dead body and another person missing."

Jacey could feel the hot tears she'd been trying to hold in check begin to run down her face. Could John really have killed this woman? What kind of monster had she been married to? Jacey knew John was a violent man. She had firsthand experience with his temper. She knew he was easily provoked, but could he have truly killed someone?

"Ms. Grayson—" Agent Parker's strong voice broke through her thoughts. "You were married to this man for nearly a decade, and you can't tell us anything?"

"No, I'm sorry. I had no idea—I never thought—" Jacey moaned. "John never discussed business with me, except for the normal, everyday things. You know, like what sort of menu they would introduce or a new restaurant that was opening. Besides those few things, John didn't tell me anything. He and Rafael always talked behind closed doors."

Agent Ronald nodded. His mouth twisted thoughtfully. "Why did you leave John Trent, Ms. Grayson?"

Jacey's eyes moved slowly to his. "John was a very violent man, and I have a nine-year-old son."

"Explain 'violent,' Ms. Grayson," Agent Parker prompted.

Jacey grimaced. She really didn't care much for Agent Parker and his brusque manner. "He was both emotionally and physically abusive. I stayed with him for far too long," Jacey replied as she wiped the stray tears off her cheeks.

"I see," Agent Parker responded with a quick glance toward his partner. "Why did you stay with him if he was violent?"

"Why does any woman stay in an abusive relationship?" Jacey could feel her temper rise. "I was scared. He threatened to take our son if I left. Besides, I always hoped he would change. Look, my son is waiting for me. I really need to go now. I'm sorry I can't be more help, but I need to go."

"Of course. Thank you for your time," Agent Parker replied, pulling a card from his coat pocket. "We'll be in touch, Ms. Grayson, and if you need anything," he waved the card, "call us anytime. Oh, just one more question, then we'll get out of your hair."

"What is that?" Jacey asked wearily.

"When was the last time you saw John Trent?"

"Six months ago, back in Chicago."

"You haven't been in contact with him since then?"

Jacey shook her head. "No. The only contact I've had with my ex-husband has been through our lawyers."

"What about your son? Trent hasn't had any contact with him since you left?"

"No, none at all. I have full custody for now."

"Does Trent know where to find you, Ms. Grayson?" Agent Ronald asked.

A tremor ran along Jacey's spine. "I hope not."

"You're frightened of him. Why?" Agent Parker questioned.

"Why shouldn't I be? I told you, he knocked me around, he had numerous affairs, and if those things you've just told me are true—then yes, I'm frightened of John. Now, if you'll excuse me, I really need to go and pick up my son. He's waiting for me."

Jacey stood weakly and moved past the two men. She could feel their eyes on her as she unlocked her car and slid into the sweltering interior. "Good day, Ms. Grayson," Agent Parker called out before she shut the door. Breathing deeply to calm her nerves, she reversed her vehicle and pulled onto the busy street.

TWO

Agent Parker watched with narrowed eyes as Jacey Grayson's vehicle pulled onto the street and melted into the late afternoon traffic.

"So," the young agent breathed. "What do we do now, Chief?" He turned to face Agent Ronald.

"Let's send in surveillance. I want someone tagging her every move. I think she knows more than she's letting on. You scared her, Agent."

"You think so?" Agent Parker chuckled. "I don't know. I think she's just traumatized by the whole situation."

"Look, rookie, you were too tough. You scared her. She wouldn't talk, even if she did know something," Agent Ronald replied, his voice gruff.

"I didn't scare her that bad, old man. Besides, I needed to rough her up a bit. She was scared, but mostly because she really didn't know anything."

"She knows something. We can't risk anything at this point. Get surveillance on her as quick as you can, Parker."

Parker grinned. "You're the boss, Chief." He chuckled as he pulled his cell phone from inside his coat.

Ronald grimaced. "That woman has to know something. We need more information on Trent and Vizcaino. Without more to go on, we can't make an arrest. They've covered their tracks too good. She's got to have something we can use."

"Maybe so. I'll get Johnston tagging her," Parker suggested.

"Johnston? He does good work. I want him out here tonight."

"Sure, but let's get out of here or go inside. I'm starving. I could smell steak and eggs the entire time we were drilling her." Parker laughed as his partner scowled.

"We've got work to do, Parker. Come on, let's get going. We have a meeting at the field office in an hour."

• • •

A surge of emotions tore through Jacey's weary body, and she tried desperately to stay calm and focused as she navigated her Jetta through the thick traffic. She had hoped to avoid this rush and, with a sinking heart, she realized that Blaze would be more than a little upset that she was late again.

"Oh," she groaned despondently as she wiped at her damp forehead. She reached with a trembling hand to increase the air conditioning. *Is John really involved in all this?*

"Yes," she whispered aloud. "He is." How could she not have seen it? John and Rafael had always been close, and Jacey had never questioned their association. Or more rightly put, she had never *dared* to question their association. Rafael had been at the house on several occasions, and Jacey had never liked the man. He scared her. Something about his silky manner and leering looks had always frightened her. Over the years, Blaze had taken to calling him Uncle Ralph. It was something Jacey had never approved of, but she had kept her disapproval to herself.

"I just can't believe it," she moaned. "But it makes sense."

John's restaurant chain had suddenly taken off once he met Rafael. Jacey had assumed it was Rafael's keen business sense that had helped John. She couldn't quite grasp it all. What sort of man had she married? He hadn't always been so heartless. When she had first met John, he had been an attractive, caring person. She couldn't help but remember how desperately she had been in love with him.

She was eighteen when they first met. Barely graduated from high school and struggling to make it on her own, she had taken a job working as a waitress in his first restaurant.

Jacey had been more lonely than usual those first several weeks after moving out of her aunt and uncle's home, where, at fourteen, she had gone to live after the death of her parents. After graduation, her aunt had been only too happy to see the last of her. Jacey had never felt welcome in their home with their three younger daughters, and as a result, she had always felt alone.

Although he was quite a bit older than Jacey, John had become her friend almost immediately. He had enjoyed teasing her and told her often how much he loved to make her laugh. She had been wary at first but as time moved on, she and John developed a close relationship, and they had dated steadily for a year before she'd become pregnant with Blaze.

At first Jacey had been frightened to tell John about her unexpected pregnancy. She felt ashamed that she had allowed herself to get into such a situation, but she had been shocked by John's reaction. He had immediately asked her to marry him. He had held her close, whispering how much he loved her and longed to share this baby together. Jacey had been swept up in the joy of his love and hadn't hesitated to accept his proposal.

Their wedding had been a memorable affair. His family had showered her with love and attention, and for the first time in a long time, Jacey finally felt as if she belonged to a family. The following months had been good for her and John. Her progressing pregnancy was exciting, and she and John had eagerly looked forward to the birth of their son.

Those days seemed surreal now. The first months together had been happy, and she couldn't have begun to imagine the extent of John's temper or how quickly her life would change.

Jacey felt tears threatening again. She had to pull herself together. She was only a block away from Blaze's school. She reached over to grab a tissue from the glove compartment and hurriedly dabbed at her damp eyes, giving herself a quick look in the rearview mirror.

"Okay," she breathed as she pulled to the curb.

She saw her son sitting on the green bench next to the double doors of the elementary school. His head was bent, his eyes focused on his shoes. He looked tired. Jacey knew he didn't sleep well at night anymore. She smiled weakly, but her heart ached for her son. She gave a quick toot on her horn to get his attention and then waved when he looked up. A frown marred his young, handsome features as he stood and grasped his worn backpack. He sluggishly made his way down the steps and into the car.

"Hey there, babe," Jacey greeted him with a smile.

"You're late, Mom," Blaze mumbled as he latched his seat belt.

"I know. I'm sorry. Honestly. I got hung up at work again." Jacey reached over to squeeze his hand. "You forgive me?" she asked, smiling a little when he turned to look at her.

"Yeah, I guess," he muttered before he turned toward his window.

Jacey sighed as she pulled out into traffic and turned her vehicle toward Melissa's neighborhood.

"How was school today?" she asked into the stretching silence.

"Okay." Blaze shrugged.

"Well," Jacey smiled encouragingly, "tell me about it."

"I dunno. I scored a goal at recess," he sighed and his eyes remained fixed out the side-window.

"Honey, that's fantastic! You'll be pro by this summer. Maybe we can get you onto Jenny's team this year," Jacey encouraged.

"Yeah. Sure."

"How did your spelling test go?"

Blaze shrugged again, and Jacey pressed, "Well, did you pass?"

"No," he muttered.

"Oh, honey. We—we worked on those words all week. You knew them by heart. What happened?"

Jacey felt her concern growing. Blaze had always done well in school up until a few months before the divorce. She knew things were hard on him, but she didn't want him to use that as an excuse to do poorly in school. "Well?" she prodded when he remained silent.

"I dunno," Blaze repeated. "I just didn't do good."

Jacey exhaled slowly, then nodded. "Okay. Do you have homework?"

Blaze nodded. "Yeah."

"What is it?"

"Science and math. Mrs. Campbell says you have to sign my test so I can take it again."

"That's good." Jacey smiled encouragingly. "We'll work on that stuff again. You'll do better this time around."

Blaze shrugged again, and Jacey worked hard to bite her tongue. He seemed to do that a lot lately—shrug. At times, she felt so frustrated with his attitude that she could scream. What was happening to her son? She just couldn't seem to break this shell that had slipped around him over the past several months. She'd had high hopes that he would get better once they were away from John, but so far he hadn't. Did he miss his father? She had tried to bring up the subject a number of times, but Blaze refused to talk about it. She knew that John scared him, but John had never touched Blaze. They had always been fairly close.

Jacey knew that her last fight with John had really affected Blaze. He'd had to go for help. Did Blaze feel guilty about turning his father in? Was he angry at Jacey for not going back to John? Jacey took a deep, trembling breath. She was getting a headache. She was scared, and she was so tired of being scared.

Silence stretched the length of the ride through the crowded subdivision. The neighborhood was teeming with activity. Children played ball in the streets and raced their bikes along the side-walks. Groups of teenagers ambled along the streets, and Jacey could hear their raucous yelling as she negotiated her way through the narrow lanes. The houses were too close together, and several were badly run down.

It was a rough neighborhood. Several of the children who lived around there had been in trouble before. But what could she do? Jacey grimaced. The city was a tough place to live, but Melissa kept a nice house. Jacey sighed with relief when she pulled the Jetta into the driveway. It wasn't home, but it was the closest thing they had to it, and it felt good to be there after such a hectic day.

"We're home." Jacey forced a smile as Blaze got out.

He slammed the car door and made a mad dash toward the

front door. "*Avatar*'s on. I'm going to miss it," he yelled as he disappeared into the house.

Jacey grabbed her purse and followed. "No, Blaze," she called as she entered the house and closed the front door. "You need to study your spelling words. No TV until you pass off those words," Jacey told him firmly, turning to switch off the television.

"Oh come on, Mom," Blaze groaned, and Jacey turned to face him.

"No." She looked into his disappointed face. She could see his frustration growing. "Into the kitchen. We have work to do."

"It's not fair!" Blaze yelled, grasping his backpack and throwing it to the floor. "I never get to watch *Avatar*. I don't care about spelling words!" He cursed loudly.

Stunned, Jacey's eyes widened. "What did you just say?"

Blaze tried to leave just as Jacey reached out to grasp his arm. She turned him to face her. "Don't talk to me like that, do you understand, Blaze? Don't you ever cuss at me. Now go into the kitchen and start on your homework. I'll—" Jacey inhaled sharply. Her eyes narrowed in frustration. "I'll be there in a minute to help you with your words. We can—"

"I don't need help, Mom," Blaze cut in. She could see his anger ebb slightly. "I'm sorry," he mumbled. Pulling his arm from her light grasp, he stomped into the kitchen.

"Can this day get any worse?" Jacey groaned as she slumped onto the sagging couch.

Her legs felt weak. The day had taxed her strength. Her mind buzzed with a flurry of memories and new worries. Blaze had seen far too much of John's temper. Should she get him into some sort of counseling? She sighed. She knew she should, but she just didn't have the funds. What was she going to do? She leaned back against the cushions, laying her head against the soft, worn pillows. She heard Blaze shuffling papers. His chair scraped, and then he coughed once. The house was quiet with only the two of them there. She could hear the clock ticking, and the sound soothed her jumbled nerves.

She felt comfortable in this house. Jacey had never really had a home since her parent's accident. She had always felt like the outsider with Uncle Jim and Aunt Kerrie. And she had never truly felt at home with John. He had always referred to everything as his. It had been his house, his vehicles, his bed, his son, and she had been his wife. How she longed for a place that she could call her own, a place where she could feel truly safe from John.

The first few months after she had left John, she and Blaze had felt safer with Melissa, but there was always the fear that John would find them. Her divorce had been handled strictly by her lawyer, and custody had been granted solely to Jacey due to the domestic violence charges.

I have custody—at least for now, she thought with a familiar jolt of fear. The idea always haunted her. John was a successful businessman, and they had always lived in the finest neighborhoods in the city and socialized with only those in his class. John was well-liked by everyone who knew him. Only Jacey and Blaze knew the real John. It was really only a matter of time before John's influence would overcome the evidence brought forward during the divorce. John would come to take Blaze away from her. The thought stole the breath from her lungs.

"Mom," Blaze's voice burst through her troubled thoughts, making her jump slightly, "Melissa and Jenny are home."

A car door slammed, and Jacey heard the thump-thump as Jenny rushed up the stairs and burst through the back door.

"Hey, guess what, Blaze?" her shrill young voice called out, echoing through the house. "The new *Batman* movie's playing at the dollar theater. Mom says she'll take us tonight!"

"Cool!" Blaze's hopeful voice rang out.

The back door slammed, and Melissa's voice joined in. "I said only if you finish your chores on time, so get busy, tart-face. Where's your mom, kiddo?" Melissa asked Blaze.

"In there," he replied abruptly. "Guess what, Jenny . . ." His young voice fell into the background as Melissa entered the living room.

"Hey you," Melissa greeted Jacey. Throwing open the closet door, she dumped her bags and purse on the floor.

"Hi," Jacey answered wearily. "How was work?"

"Work . . . hmm." Melissa snorted as she came around the

couch. "You mean the sweat shop? Oh fine, I suppose." She grinned as she eyed Jacey. "What about you, girl? You look like you've had a tough day."

Jacey laughed humorlessly and then slumped back against the couch. "You could say that." She exhaled loudly.

"Something wrong?" Melissa asked. "You look haggard."

"Gee, thanks, Missy." She smiled.

Melissa grinned. "No, really, girl. What's wrong?"

Jacey shook her head. She sat up and eyed the doorway that led to the kitchen. She could hear the kids' muffled voices and wrappers shuffling as they rummaged through the snack cupboard. She turned to face Melissa, all traces of humor gone.

"It's John," she admitted, her voice low. Melissa's eyes narrowed, and she nodded for her to go on. "Today after work, two FBI agents stopped me. They told me a lot of things about John. He's—Melissa, he—" Jacey stopped to collect her thoughts.

"He's what, Jace?" Melissa pressed.

"They said he and Rafael Vizcaino are suspected of money laundering and drug trafficking. They also think that John and Rafael might be behind some attorney's murder back in Chicago."

"What?" Melissa breathed, astounded. "They think he's a murderer? Wow." She whistled quietly.

Jacey nodded. "They think he might have killed this woman, and possibly another man named Gary Walbeck. He's that journalist that's disappeared."

"You're kidding!" Melissa's eyes widened with surprise. "I've heard about that. What did they want with you?"

Jacey shook her head. "I don't know exactly. I think—I think they believe I know something about it. For a minute I thought they were trying to accuse me of killing this woman. They said she and John had an affair."

"Doesn't surprise me," Melissa said. "What do they think you know?"

"I don't know. They seemed surprised that I didn't know anything. It was such a huge shock. I can hardly believe it. I never—I don't know what to do, Melissa," Jacey admitted. She tucked her trembling hands beneath her legs and sat forward. "I have this feeling that Blaze and I are in danger. I think John might come after us. I think he and Rafael will come after me for taking Blaze," Jacey whispered.

"Did you tell the FBI that you didn't know anything?" Melissa asked with a quick glance toward the kitchen.

"Of course I told them, but I don't think they believed me."

Melissa grimaced as she moved to the couch and sat next to Jacey. At any other time, her bewildered expression would have been almost comical, but it frightened Jacey. What was she going to do?

"What—?" Melissa began just as Jenny's voice interrupted from the kitchen.

"Mom," Jenny called as she popped her head around the doorway. "Can we have a donut?"

"Sure," Melissa responded brusquely. "Now go do your chores. Your bedroom is a disaster zone."

"I will, Mom. Good grief," Jenny groaned as she backed into the kitchen.

"Do you really think John would think to look for you here?" Melissa whispered.

Jacey shrugged, frustrated. "The FBI found me. Why not John? If the FBI is right about him, I think he could."

Melissa nodded. "Then let's go to the police."

"The FBI suspects that I know something. They may even think I'm involved, Melissa. The police aren't going to protect me, and besides, look how often ex-wives are tracked down and killed despite 'police protection.' John was so angry that I took Blaze. I think—I think Blaze and I need to leave."

"And go where?" Melissa's voice rose a fraction. "You don't have family. Well, except for your uncle's family. John could trace you just as easily to them as he could to us."

"I know," Jacey muttered, leaning her head into her trembling hands. Her headache intensified.

"You're white as a ghost, Jace." Melissa put a comforting arm around Jacey's shoulder and squeezed. "I'll go get you some water and a couple of aspirin, maybe a donut if the kids haven't eaten them all."

"Thanks," Jacey mumbled as Melissa disappeared into the kitchen.

She was very grateful for Melissa's strength. Melissa had always been Jacey's rock. They had met several years ago when Jenny and Blaze had been in the same class back in Chicago. They had become fast friends. Over the years, Melissa had pleaded with Jacey to leave John, but Jacey had never had the courage to do it. Then, after Melissa's divorce, Melissa had again begged Jacey to move to Detroit with her and Jenny, but Jacey had refused, still clinging to the small chance that John could change.

"Did you eat them all?" Jacey could hear Melissa's muffled voice coming from the kitchen. "Give me one of those, you little twerps. You know, you could eat a woman out of house and home." Melissa's voice grew louder as she reentered the living room, and Jacey heard the kids laugh.

Melissa came around and sat on the coffee table to face Jacey. "Here, take these," Melissa ordered softly, handing Jacey two aspirin and a donut. "Enjoy this while you can. It's the last one. Those little piggies ate almost the whole box. I had to go in with gnashing teeth and claws to save this one."

Jacey chuckled. "Thanks, Melissa. I can always count on you."

"Oh, don't get all sentimental on me now." Melissa winked. "Listen, we'll think of something, girl. There's always something. Try not to worry, all right?"

Jacey sighed and a soft smile touched her lips. "You're right. Let's go help those kids with their work. I've been dying to see that new *Batman* movie."

THREE

Jacey moaned as the loud, piercing beep of her alarm clock roused her from a restless sleep. In a daze she sought out the clock next to the bed and hit the snooze button. Then she flopped back against the squeaky mattress with another loud groan. Her body ached from stress, and she could still feel the remnants of her headache from yesterday. She needed to get up and get ready for work, but the thought of spending another long Saturday at the café did nothing to encourage her. She lay there for a few more moments. Her mind drifted back to thoughts of yesterday, of John, and of Blaze.

She moaned into the silence of the morning. She had to get away from Melissa's before John found her. What she needed was a day to just think. She needed a day to spend with Blaze. Maybe things wouldn't seem so ominous if she could just have time to relax. Jacey knew Ian would be raving mad, but she had to stay home. Blaze needed her, and she needed Blaze. Ian would get over it eventually, and besides, she needed the extra sleep after a night like she'd just had. Determined, Jacey pulled her weary body from the bed and wobbled downstairs to find her cell phone. She would call Ian and then catch a few more hours of much-needed sleep. Then later—much later—she and Blaze would go to the zoo. It would be their first adventure together in a long time.

• • •

Agent Ronald blew out a frustrated breath as he pushed himself away from his desk and the never-ending pile of paperwork. Things were moving too slowly with this case. He needed more information on the Vizcaino crime ring before another body was found. He had been investigating Vizcaino's moderate organization for nearly two years. With help from the inside, Ronald had been able to make a few arrests, but this was the first time he had ever been so close to shutting down the operation altogether. He just needed to find the right pieces of the puzzle. A few more bits of solid evidence and he could shut Rafael and his cronies up for a long time.

Ronald stood to stretch his long legs. He felt stiff and sore. He was starting to feel his age. It would be nice to wrap this case up so he could relax a little. Maybe he would finally be able to take that fishing trip with his brother.

He and Clark had planned that trip for nearly five years, but something had always come up. Bagging Vizcaino and Trent would leave his schedule open for a least a few weeks. If only he could get something on Jacey Grayson. There had to be something. She couldn't have been married to a jerk like John Trent for eight years and not know anything. He grimaced and turned to face the window. The streets were packed today, and the thick July heat seemed to suffocate the thriving city. He groaned at the thought of returning to his desk. He hated paperwork, always had.

"Hey, Chief," Agent Parker's voice called through the doorway of the cramped office. Ronald turned to watch as his young partner, holding several thick folders, ambled through the door.

"If that's more paperwork for me, I'm throwing you out that window." Ronald scowled, turning back to his desk.

"No worries, boss. This is mine." Parker laughed at the older man's expression. "But hey, I've got some good news. Well, maybe not good news, but its news."

"What?" Ronald asked, slumping into his worn desk chair. He swiveled around to face his tower of work.

"Johnston's been tagging Jacey Grayson. I told you I could get him down here quick," Parker replied, pulling a chair to the other side of Ronald's desk.

"Well? So what's going on with surveillance?" Ronald asked gruffly.

"Nothing much. So far she and her boy went to the zoo. It turned out to be a nice little outing. They ate ice cream and stopped at a fast food joint for lunch. They went to a couple of stores and now, last I'd heard, they've been in the rest of the afternoon." Parker laughed at Ronald's annoyed expression.

"I thought you said you had news. That isn't news, rookie," he growled.

"Hey, the good news was that I got Johnston. Sorry if a trip to the zoo wasn't filled with mystery and mayhem, but it's like this: I think the woman's clean. I believed her when she said she didn't know anything."

Ronald scowled. "You just make sure Johnston and his men keep her and Trent's boy in sight at all times, you hear? There's always the possibility Trent may approach them. And besides, we've got to look at all angles if we're ever going to bag this case. Got it?"

"Got it, Chief. I'll take care of it." Parker smirked as he pushed away from the desk. "I need a soda. Want me to pick one up for you? You look like you need it."

"Yeah, sure," Ronald mumbled, turning back to his work. If he didn't get busy now, he would be in the office all night.

• • •

"I hate that word," Blaze said. "When am I ever going to use 'acquainted'? Honestly, Mom."

Jacey laughed as her son attempted to spell the word again. "No, Blaze. It's 'A-C-Q-U. Remember a U always comes after the Q. And honestly, you'll use that word more than once as you get older, babe. Now come on. Concentrate. The sooner you pass these words off, the sooner you can get *acquainted* with that TV again."

"All right, all right," he moaned. "Hey, Mom, remember that goat today? You know the one that kept hitting the fence? I can't wait to tell Jenny about it. That was a mean goat, and it was ugly too." Blaze laughed.

"It was. I wouldn't want that thing to get loose, that's for certain. Okay, now how do you spell 'knowledgeable'?"

"Aw, Mom," Blaze groaned.

Jacey had to turn and hide her smile. She and Blaze had really had a great day. The zoo, although a little too hot for comfort, had been such a new adventure for the two of them. Blaze had gone to the Lincoln Park Zoo once or twice when they'd lived in Chicago, but only with his school class. Today's trip had been a fun experience for the two of them.

"What're you cooking, Mom?" Blaze asked lazily. He tipped his chair back on two legs.

Jacey eyed him with feigned disgust. "You're going to break that chair."

"No I won't. I do it all the time at school," Blaze responded, his voice rising defensively.

"That isn't a school chair, Blaze. It's Melissa's chair, and she's not going to be very happy when she comes home and sees you've broken it," Jacey replied. She pointed at his papers scattered about the tabletop. "Come on now, back to work."

"But I'm too hungry to spell," Blaze whined. He clutched his stomach with an exaggerated groan, just as the back door was suddenly thrown open.

"Hey, Blaze," Jenny hollered as she rushed into the kitchen. "Hi, Aunt Jacey. Whattcha cookin'?"

"Sloppy Joes," Jacey responded with a smile. She turned to give the energetic girl a quick hug. "Hungry?"

"Yessss," Jenny breathed loudly, "I'm starving."

"You're always starving, toots," Melissa's voice joined in as she stepped through the door. "Hi, you two. Did you have a good day?"

"It was great." Jacey laughed as she stirred the sauce.

"Yeah," Blaze said, "we saw tons of things, and there was this little, evil goat that kept trying to bite me over the fence."

"Really?" Melissa laughed. "Hey, Jacey, we need to talk, babe."

Jacey turned to face her friend. "Yeah?"

"Sure do. All right, twerps! Upstairs so we adults can talk."

Melissa indicated the stairs with an exaggerated wave of her hand.

"Aw no, Mom," Jenny whined.

"All right! No more spelling!" Blaze grinned, jumping away from the table. "Come on, Jenny, let's go."

"Fine," Jenny said before she and Blaze disappeared up the narrow stairs.

"So what is it, Missy?" Jacey asked, stirring the sauce one final time before coming around to sit at the table.

"Listen, girl," Melissa whispered, leaning closer to Jacey. "I had the most brain-boggling idea today. I think I just might know where you and Blaze can go to hide from John for a while. I've thought about it all day, and I think it'll work."

Jacey looked doubtful as she asked, "What is it?"

"This is great," Melissa began. "My dad's brother and his wife live in some little town out in Utah. I've actually never met them, although we have exchanged letters before—well, when I was younger anyways. So my dad and my uncle never really got along as far as I know. Then when Uncle Grant and Aunt Helen joined up with the Mormons—well, Dad never had much to do with him after that.

"Aunt Helen and Mom wrote to each other through the years, and Aunt Helen and Uncle Grant always wanted to meet me, but Dad refused. I haven't heard from them for several years, probably not since before Jenny was born. We sort of lost touch after Dad was killed in the accident. But I checked it all out. They're both still alive, and they live in a place called Mona or something like that. So it's perfect," Melissa finished with triumphant smile.

Jacey's wide eyes narrowed. "So *what's* perfect, Melissa?"

"Don't you get it?" Melissa asked. "You can go there—as me!"

Jacey's mouth fell open. Was Melissa serious? She shook her head, bewildered, as Melissa went on.

"They've never seen me in person, only in pictures. You and I look so similar they'll never guess after all these years. And there's no way on earth John would go looking for two of me."

"That's . . . crazy!" Jacey replied slowly. Melissa couldn't be serious. "I can't do that! It would never work. How do you know they would even welcome Blaze and me? And besides, you have a daughter, Missy, remember?"

"Of course I remember. I already took care of all that. I called them."

"Are—are you nuts?" Jacey staggered breathlessly. "You called them?"

"I did. I told them that my son and I needed a break from this horrible city heat, and they were both ecstatic over the idea. I told them that I would be out there by next Friday. That should give you and Blaze enough time to straighten things out with summer school and work, get packed, and then drive to Utah. I hate to see you drive all that way, but John could trace a plane ticket under your name pretty easy," Melissa reasoned.

Silence filled the kitchen as Melissa watched Jacey with restrained expectancy. Bewildered, Jacey fell back against her chair and anxiously tucked a long strand of auburn hair behind her ear.

"Melissa," she began, "I—well, this—how can I do this? It's crazy! And it just doesn't seem right. What would I tell Blaze? What if they figured it out? How could I deceive your family like that? It seems so wrong."

"Jacey," Melissa encouraged, "you and Blaze need to get away from here before John finds you, right? John is a terrible man, Jacey. You have to believe that. I don't like the thought of deceiving Uncle Grant and Aunt Helen either, but what can it hurt? It'll only be for a little while, until you and Blaze can find a place to stay. Desperate times call for desperate measures, Jace. Besides, it'll be easy. I'll drill you on everything that could possibly come up, and we'll rehearse. It'll be an adventure."

"I know I've got to get away, Melissa, but this seems so . . . wrong."

"What's so wrong? So you pretend to be me for a week or two, big deal. You can do it. Girl, you can't just pick up and leave with no place to go. You need a safe place to stay until you can figure things out. I don't want you to leave, but if John—"

"I know, I know," Jacey cut in. "I've been a nervous wreck. Ever since yesterday I've had this awful feeling about John.

But what am I going to tell Blaze?" Jacey asked. Her voice trembled.

"The truth," Melissa reached over to clasp one of Jacey's hands. "He's nine years old, and if you ask me, he's seen far more than any nine-year-old should ever see. He's a smart boy. Chances are he's going to understand, Jacey. He sees and understands more than you realize," Melissa reminded her gently.

Jacey shook her head. "I don't know what to say. We've really got no other choice, I suppose."

"It'll work, Jace. You and Blaze have to stay safe, and you won't be anymore—not here. John has to know where you are by now. And if he doesn't, well, it's only a matter of time, right?"

Jacey nodded. She ran a hand across her face before she reached over to embrace Melissa. "I know, and thank you," she whispered. Her voice cracked with emotion.

Melissa's arms tightened around Jacey's slim shoulders just as Jenny's voice called from above, "Can we come down yet? We're wasting away up here, Mom."

"Good grief. All right, you can come down now," she called to Jenny. Then, with a quick look to Jacey, she whispered hurriedly, "You can explain everything to Blaze tonight. We'll work out all the kinks later. It'll be fine."

• • •

Jacey sighed as she glanced toward the living room. Blaze and Jenny had turned the lights out, and Jacey could see the bright flashes of illumination reflecting off the walls.

Melissa caught the direction of Jacey's glance and then whispered, "Now's as good a time as any, girl. I'll finish up the dishes. Oh, and send Jenny in. She still has chores to finish. I'll make her finish the dishes."

"Sure," Jacey said, grinning, "send me to do the hard part."

"Just threaten to hide her *Pokemon* cards. It works wonders. I swear—*Pokemon*? What's happened to the good old stuff?"

Jacey shook her head, smiling a little. "Thanks, Melissa. I'll send her right in." She dried her hands before she walked slowly into the living room.

"Hey, you two," Jacey greeted Blaze and Jenny as she flipped on the light.

"Hi," they said in unison without a glance her way.

"Jenny, your mom wants you in the kitchen, pronto." Jacey lightly touched Jenny's shoulder.

"Aw . . . but I was—"

"She said to threaten you with your Pokemon cards." Jacey winked.

Jenny grimaced. "Oh, fine," she mumbled as she stood and sauntered into the kitchen. Blaze grinned before turning back to the show.

"Blaze," Jacey began uncertainly, "why don't you turn off the television? You and I need to talk for a minute, all right?"

Blaze's eyes shot to hers. "Okay," he responded slowly, and Jacey was surprised to catch a fleeting look of fear in his dark eyes before he moved to switch off the television. Jacey eyed him with concern before Blaze asked, "What, Mom?"

She sighed. "Come sit down." Jacey said, scooting over on the sofa to make room next to her. "Blaze, I don't know how to tell you this, but you and I need to go away for a little while. We—"

"We can't live here anymore?" Blaze interrupted.

"Not right now, no." She sucked in a deep breath and went on, "Blaze, I know you've been through a lot over the last several months with the divorce. I don't like to have to tell you these things, but you're getting older, and well, honey, I've—well, I've learned some things about your dad that have me worried."

Blaze's eyes widened. She could read the panic building in his expression, and Jacey went on quickly. "It's nothing, really, but I worry that your dad might try to find us, and he might try to take you away from me. We can't let Dad find us right now. Melissa has an aunt and uncle who live in Utah, and well, things are sort of complicated with the whole situation. I'll explain it all, but you and I are going to go and stay with them for a little while. Just until I know we can be safe from your dad. All right?"

Blaze ducked his head, and Jacey could see his hands tremble slightly. "Kay," he whispered.

"Blaze, you do understand why it's so important for your dad not to find us right now?" Jacey asked, taking one of his hands in hers.

Blaze nodded slightly. "He'll kill you." His eyes filled with tears.

"Oh, Blaze," she gasped, reaching for him. Her arms came about him tightly, and she pulled his thin frame against her. "Honey, no. Oh no. Your dad wouldn't kill me. He just lost control that day. He wasn't trying—he wouldn't have killed me. He should have never lost control the way he did, and it was very wrong of him to hurt me."

Jacey groaned inwardly and pulled her son's trembling body closer. *What have I done to my son?* she thought, angry at herself for staying with John so long and subjecting her son to his abuse.

"Dad and Uncle Ralph are really bad people," Blaze mumbled against Jacey's shoulder.

Startled, Jacey pulled away to look into his haunted eyes. "Why do you say that, Blaze?" she asked quietly. Her heart pounded against her ribs. Blaze quickly ducked his head to hide his fear. "Blaze, did your dad and Uncle Ralph do something that scared you? Do you need to tell me something, honey?" she asked. A shiver ran the length of her spine.

"No," Blaze responded, shaking his head. He leaned back against her shoulder, and Jacey's arms tightened around him.

"You know you can tell me anything, right, Blaze? If Dad and Uncle Ralph did something that scared you, you need to tell me," she persisted.

Blaze shook his head against her shoulder and sniffed loudly, "No, I just don't want him to hurt you again. I don't want Dad to take me away."

She relaxed slightly. "I'll never let that happen, Blaze. Not ever." Jacey squeezed him tight and leaned her head in against his. She breathed in the scent of his shampoo and nuzzled her face into his soft hair. She would never let that man take her son. Determined, Jacey knew she would do whatever it took to protect her boy, even if it meant going to Utah as Melissa.

FOUR

"Mom, I'm hungry," Blaze's voice suddenly cut across the radio.

A smile hovered on Jacey's lips. "We just ate lunch a couple hours ago."

"I know, but I'm hungry again." Blaze moaned, teasing, and Jacey grinned.

"You're that hungry?"

"Uh-huh," Blaze groaned again.

"Okay, okay, we'll take the next exit and get a soda or something. We probably need to get some gas anyway."

"Can I pump?" Blaze asked, his voice hopeful.

"Sure," Jacey responded. "You can help."

Blaze grinned and turned back toward the window. "This is weird out here, Mom. It looks like Mars or something." He waved his hand toward the red dirt and sandstone plateaus. "Is this what it's going to look like when we get to—umm, what's it called?"

"Mona, honey, and I don't think so. It does look strange. I like it though. It looks so different from anything I've ever seen."

Jacey sighed. She focused on the road ahead. It seemed to stretch on for miles. The landscape did look like something out of a sci-fi movie. They had just left Grand Junction, Colorado, and Jacey knew they would be entering Utah soon. Her nervousness only increased the closer they got. They had taken a much longer route than normal, just to be safe, and she and Blaze had spent the better part of two days on the road.

"How much longer before we get there?" Blaze asked.

"We'll probably make it by this evening," Jacey responded with a quick glance in his direction.

His brow furrowed, and he nodded silently before turning back to face the window.

"It'll be fine." Jacey sighed softly. "And don't bite your finger-nails," she added when she noticed Blaze's fingers in his mouth.

He'd had that habit since he was very young. Jacey knew Blaze was extremely nervous, and she hoped that they could really pull this off. What if she blew it? What if Blaze made a mistake? He was only nine, and she was asking so much of him.

"Do you remember what we talked about?" Jacey asked Blaze, feeling a sudden urge to rehearse it all again.

"Yeah," he said.

"Well, let's go over it again, okay? Just to be safe."

"I can't tell people your real name. You're Melissa McCoy. I'm Blaze McCoy. And we're going to stay with Uncle Grant and Aunt Helen. I know, I know," Blaze replied. "Hey, what about school, Mom?"

"You won't go to school for now. Summer school is going to be out in two weeks anyway, and besides, I don't think they have year-round school in Utah. I think their school year starts in August. Hopefully by then we'll be in our own place. Then things can get back to normal," Jacey replied with an inward grimace. Since when had anything been normal for Blaze?

"What about your job, Mom?"

"I've got some savings for now, and I'll worry about another job in a couple of weeks."

"Do Uncle Grant and Aunt Helen really live on a farm?"

"That's what Melissa told me," Jacey replied.

Blaze grinned. "You're Melissa. Remember, Mom?"

She laughed. "Oh yeah. Well then, that's what *I* said. Thanks, babe."

"Do you think they've got horses and cows?" he questioned curiously.

"I'm sure they do. Horses, cows, maybe chickens and pigs. I'm not sure, but it's a farm, so they've got to have some sort of animal."

"Maybe it's a mink farm." Blaze giggled when Jacey pulled a "yuck" face.

"I hope not."

"Do you think if they have horses, Uncle Grant will let me ride them? Jenny got to ride a real big horse when they went to the fair last year."

"I bet he will, if they have horses."

"Tomorrow?" Blaze asked. His expression brightened.

Jacey laughed. It was good to see him interested in something besides those obnoxious cartoons he always watched on television. "Well, I don't know about tomorrow, but if he has horses, I'm sure he'll teach you soon."

"I hope he does. Are they nice, Mom?"

Jacey glanced toward her son. His eyes suddenly grew apprehensive. "They sound very nice," she responded with a quick smile. "I talked to Uncle Grant yesterday morning. They seem very excited to meet us."

"Really?" Blaze sounded doubtful.

"Really, Blaze," she replied with an encouraging grin. "They both sound like wonderful people."

Blaze nodded before he turned once again to face the window.

Jacey sighed, remembering the conversation she'd had with the older man. He had sounded genuinely pleased at the prospect of Melissa and her son's visit. Even over the phone, Jacey had found the deception difficult. It felt so out of character for her to lie.

Melissa had briefed Jacey on everything that might come up in any conversation with the older couple, and Jacey felt fairly comfortable that she could remember everything Melissa had told her. They had reviewed everything from Melissa's parents and their relationship clear through Melissa's divorce with Spencer. Everything since Jenny's birth would be fairly easy to pull off, since Melissa's last contact with her aunt and uncle had been long before that. Jacey groaned inwardly. She hoped desperately that she could do this. She and Blaze had to make this work, somehow.

She had decided they would stay a week or two. Just long enough for her to devise a plan for their future. If they liked Utah, it would be the best place to stay. She felt fairly certain that John would never think of Utah. She had grown up on the East Coast, and she and John had only ever lived in Chicago. Salt Lake City sounded promising, and she felt confident she could find work in the city and a place for her and Blaze to settle down. If she and Blaze could just survive the next couple of weeks, Jacey knew they would be all right.

• • •

"Blaze, wake up, babe," Jacey called out as she neared the exit to Mona from I-15. Her stomach clenched, and she reached over to gently shake her son. "Wake up, honey," she said again.

Blaze stirred before he slowly opened his sleepy eyes. "Are we there?" he mumbled wearily.

"No, but we're getting real close." She hoped he couldn't hear the tremor in her voice.

Blaze coughed, then sat up to gaze out toward the darkening sky. "What time is it, Mom?" he asked with a wide yawn.

"Almost nine-thirty. I hope they don't mind us getting here so late," she mumbled mostly to herself.

Blaze eyed Jacey nervously as she exited the freeway and headed into the sparsely populated town. Jacey had never seen such a large extent of wide-open spaces. There had been no cities or even larger buildings to speak of for miles. It was a strange thing to see the various little towns scattered along the freeway. They had just passed through a place called Nephi, which seemed to be about the largest town around. Jacey knew from a map that Provo was the nearest city to Mona, and it was still a fair distance away.

"This is Mona?" Blaze asked. He rolled down his window. "It smells funny, Mom."

Jacey laughed nervously. "Maybe it's cows?"

Blaze nodded but didn't respond. Jacey reached over to grasp his hand. She squeezed his cold fingers between hers. "Everything will be fine, babe. You'll see. This will be the hardest part," she reminded him.

"What if they don't like us?" he questioned warily.

Jacey smiled at her son through the fading light. "They'll love us. Besides, who couldn't love you?"

"Come on, Mom," Blaze scowled and turned away.

"Try not to worry, honey. Everything will be fine," she repeated. She hoped she was right.

Silent apprehension filled the car as they approached the small, sleepy town. Following the instructions Grant had given her, she turned left near the café and drove down the quiet streets of Mona. One or two cars joined hers on the road as she drove toward the newer section of the small city. New houses were being built next to the road and down across the open expanse of fields. Lights shone from several homes as she drove on toward the edge of town.

"I think maybe that's it," Jacey could see the lights of a few scattered houses beyond the town in the distance. Two in particular were set far back against a dark hill. "It's got to be one of those," she told Blaze. "Uncle Grant said they lived back toward the hills."

"They live clear out here?" Blaze sat up and gazed toward the lights that glinted in the distance.

"Help me find a sign that says 'Jackman.' It should be along this main road. We need to find the road that goes out toward those houses," Jacey replied.

"I think that's it," Blaze pointed ahead as the Jetta's bright lights reflected off a metal sign several feet ahead of them.

As they approached, Jacey shook her head. "No, that isn't it."

"Oh, that says 'Barnes.'" Blaze pointed toward the sign, and Jacey slowed down nervously.

The road had to be close. She squinted through the falling darkness, then breathed a sigh of relief when she spotted a large wooden post with "Jackman" written down its length several feet away.

"There it is. Grant said to pass this first house, so it's got to be that house back there."

She turned down the narrow dirt lane leading toward the Jackman's farm. "Well," she forced a smile, "here goes nothing."

Blaze remained silent, his eyes fixed on the lights ahead. Jacey wished she could do or say something to relieve his insecurity, but as they drew ever nearer, her own nerves seemed to stand on end. Blowing out a shaky breath, Jacey rolled down her window. The crisp air calmed her raging nerves, and she breathed in the fresh, musky scent before she glanced at Blaze. The bright lights from the dashboard reflected off the left side of his young face, and Jacey could clearly read his discomfort.

"Blaze," she began, her voice low, "I wish we didn't have to lie to these people, but right now we desperately need a place to stay. We need a place to hide from your father until we know it's safe."

His eyes remained fixed ahead. "I know," he said.

Jacey reached over to pull his hand into hers. She smiled, gently squeezing his fingers.

"I'm okay, Mom." He pulled his hand away.

Jacey nodded and held her breath as they neared the house. She turned into a circular gravel drive. The outside lights illuminated the two-story rambler. Jacey gripped the wheel tightly as she came to a stop in front of a wide porch. She eyed the house apprehensively. It was different from what she had imagined. Come to think of it, she wasn't sure what she had expected, but the cream and brown house looked inviting. The large wooden porch framed the house nicely, and the soft lights that shone from the windows left Jacey longing, unexpectedly, for the memory of a real home.

"Is this the only house out here?" Blaze asked uncertainly.

"No, there's the house we passed back by the main road. Look," she pointed down the road in the direction they had just come. "And I saw another house behind this one, further past those fields."

Jacey squinted and tried to look past the lights of the house. She could make out the dark shadows of a large fence, but beyond that, the night was too thick.

"You ready?" she asked as she opened her door.

The cool night air surrounded her weary body as Jacey left the comfort and security of her car. She moaned quietly, stretching her stiff muscles. She had spent too many hours behind the wheel. She raised a hand to her neck and absently rubbed the aching muscles, turning to face the house. She heard the crunch of gravel when Blaze got out of the car and stood to face her, his expression a mask of uncertainty. She smiled, hoping to reassure him, just as the front door creaked open and light spilled onto the porch.

"Melissa, you're here," Jacey heard a soft voice call just as a plump figure filled the doorway.

Jacey took an awkward step forward while Blaze moved closer to the car. The woman walked onto the porch, and Jacey quickly took in her appearance—gray hair pulled into a messy bun at the back of her head, faded jeans, and a large flower-patterned blouse. The woman smiled openly as she hurried down the steps toward Jacey.

"Hi . . . Aunt Helen?" Jacey greeted the woman hesitantly.

"I'm so glad you've made it safe."

Aunt Helen came forward and gathered Jacey into a tight embrace. Jacey stiffened but placed her arms around the plump woman. Aunt Helen smelt like cookies, and Jacey couldn't help but smile a little.

"You made it." Uncle Grant suddenly appeared on the porch.

Jacey's eyes widened with surprise as Grant moved closer. He was tall—and big. Jacey hadn't known what to expect, but this man towered over herself and Helen.

"We were wondering if you would get here soon." He approached her with a broad grin.

"Hi, Uncle Grant." Jacey looked up toward the older man. "I'm so glad to finally meet you."

"I'm glad you came." Grant suddenly jerked Jacey into a tight embrace. He held her for a moment before he pulled back awkwardly. "I'm so glad you've come." Grant's voice filled with checked emotion. "My family—my brother's daughter."

"Oh," Jacey mumbled, "I—" *What am I supposed to say?*

"You must be Blaze." He moved past Jacey, and she breathed a sigh of relief as all attention turned to her son. Jacey stepped back and grasped Blaze's elbow.

"Yes, this is Blaze," Jacey introduced him. She could feel Blaze stiffen as he moved closer to her.

"I'm Aunt Helen, and this big brute is Uncle Grant." Helen reached out and grasped Blaze's hand.

"Hi," Blaze mumbled timidly.

Uncle Grant moved closer and placed a thick arm around Helen's shoulders before he bent low and eyed Blaze with a wide smile. Blaze shrank further into Jacey's side. Feeling embarrassed, Jacey gave him a quick nudge.

"I've got something special that I've been saving just for you, young man." Grant's eyes twinkled.

"What—what is it?" Blaze mumbled. He eyed Grant cautiously.

"Well," Grant stood and squeezed Helen's shoulders tenderly, "come and have a look for yourself, boy."

Blaze's eyes caught Jacey's, and he reached for her hand.

"Well, let's go see," Jacey replied. She smiled awkwardly at Grant and Helen.

"Come on, then." Helen turned toward the house while Blaze and Jacey followed.

From the porch they entered the small living area. The house smelt like freshly baked cookies, and its cheery warmth immediately greeted Jacey. She glanced around the small living area. The carpet was worn but clean, and the furniture, though aged, looked inviting. An antique piano sat against the far side of the living room, and rustic, Western-type paintings adorned the walls. A worn oak floor led from the living room into the dining room past a steep set of stairs.

"Do you see it?" Grant asked with a smile as he ushered Jacey and Blaze into the cozy living space.

"Have a seat." Helen indicated the soft couch.

"Well, son, what do you think?" Grant interjected.

Blaze looked around the room curiously before his eyes fell on a saddle sitting on the piano bench. His eyes widened with excitement, and he moved hesitantly toward the saddle. Jacey sat down on the sofa. She eyed the shiny saddle with a smile, and Blaze's expression brightened. He reached out a hand to touch the saddle horn. Jacey could smell the freshly oiled leather.

"Do you think you'd like to learn to ride, boy?" Grant asked, moving to sit next to Helen.

Blaze turned toward Grant, his eyes wide. "Really? That's for me?" he asked.

Jacey could read the anticipation in her son's expression.

"It is. I found that yesterday, out in the tack shed. It used to belong to my boy, Kale. He used that when he was just about your age. Think we could put it to good use again?" Grant laughed when Blaze's face split into a grin, and he nodded eagerly.

"I *knew* they'd have horses," Blaze informed Jacey as he examined his new gift. "Can we go tomorrow?" he added.

"Blaze," Jacey admonished softly.

"I don't see why not." Grant laughed and winked at Jacey.

Jacey smiled quickly to cover her embarrassment. "He's been so excited to ride a horse. He'll love it. Thank you."

"It looks like a real cowboy saddle," Blaze told Jacey. "See." He pointed toward the stirrups.

Grant guffawed loudly. "Well, it is a real cowboy's saddle, boy."

Blaze grinned sheepishly as he turned toward Helen and Grant. "Thanks a whole lot."

"Glad you like it, and oh—" Grant turned to Helen—"We almost forgot." He eyed Helen with a meaningful smile, and Helen's eyes popped wide with sudden understanding.

"Good heavens, we *did* almost forget." She laughed as she rose from the couch and rushed into the dining room. She returned almost immediately, her hands behind her back. "You can't ride a horse without one of these." She came toward Blaze, pulling a white, wide-brimmed, straw cowboy hat from behind her back.

"That's for me?" Blaze asked, his voice filled with wonder.

Helen reached out to place the hat on his head. "It fits. I was worried." She turned toward Jacey with a smile.

"Wow, Mom! Look at this. It's a real cowboy hat." Blaze adjusted the hat and turned toward the older couple. "This is cool. Thanks! I can't wait till tomorrow."

Grant chuckled boisterously and replied, "We had our son Kale pick up the hat in the city day before yesterday. You'll probably have a chance to meet him tomorrow. He lives in that big house further back. He had business in Salt Lake today so he stayed up there for the night. He should be back first thing in the morning, though."

"Thank you so much. This is really nice," Jacey replied, already beginning to feel more comfortable.

Helen beamed. "Well, we're just so happy to have you here."

"Sure are," Grant's deep voice joined in. "You don't know what it means to have my family here."

Jacey nodded. "Well, we're really glad to be here. It's great to finally meet you both."

"So," Helen smiled and stood, "would you like to see the house?"

"Oh, yes. Yes, we would love to." Jacey stood, grateful for the chance to avoid an awkward conversation. She had immediately liked Grant and Helen, and now, more than ever, the idea of deceiving them was becoming a terrible burden.

"Coming?" Jacey asked Blaze. He moved next to her, his new hat still sitting firmly on his head.

Grant followed as Helen led them through the dining room and into a small charming kitchen. The yellow daisy wallpaper made the room feel bright and sunny. Colorful rag rugs covered the distressed wood floors, and a vase of yellow artificial flowers decorated the counter. The chocolate chip cookie smell was even stronger here, and Jacey's stomach growled.

"This is nice," Jacey said. "It feels so comfortable."

"Thank you, dear. Now, that's the washroom, and right through there is the back door." Helen pointed to a small screened-in area just off the kitchen. "And anything you need, you just help yourselves to it. I keep the snacks in the pantry over there, and I hide all the cookies in that cupboard. I hope you and Blaze like cookies."

"I do!" Blaze jumped in.

Grant laughed. "So do I. We'll have to try to sneak some before bed."

"Oh no, you don't." Helen turned with a mock glare toward her husband. "I made those special for Blaze and Melissa. You just keep your hands off, Mr. Jackman." Helen smiled. "He'd eat every one if I'd let him," she told Jacey and Blaze.

"She has me on one of those terrible 'women' diets," Grant whispered. Blaze giggled.

"Now, let me show you upstairs. All the bedrooms are on the second level," Helen informed them cheerfully as she led the way toward the steep staircase.

Several photographs adorned the walls at the top of the stairs. A younger Grant and Helen smiled out from some of the glass frames as well as a smiling boy, who she guessed was their son, Kale, and an attractive girl, who looked much like Helen.

"Our room is just down the hall. There, at the end." Helen pointed toward a closed door. "We put you and Blaze across from one another. The bathroom's there." Helen indicated another door with a flick of her hand before leading them into the room next to it. "This is going to be your room, Blaze."

Jacey couldn't help but gasp as she and Blaze entered the room. A large knotty-pine bed filled the space. The tan and brown comforter looked warm and clean, and several large pillows were propped neatly against the headboard. Pictures of horses adorned the walls, and a tall bookshelf, filled to capacity, leaned against the far wall. A small television sat below the window, and two large tree stumps worked as the bed stands. One held a lamp, made of shiny twisted wood, while a few books, held upright by polished rocks, sat on the other. Jacey had never seen a room quite like it.

"Cool," Blaze said behind Jacey.

"This room was Kale's," Grant put in.

"That's an awesome bed," Blaze responded.

"You like that? Kale made it when he was a boy in high school."

"That's very impressive," Jacey replied sincerely. She smiled as she watched her son eagerly explore the room.

"He's got a lot of cool rocks." Blaze pointed to the top of the dresser.

Several rocks were displayed in a shallow, cratelike box, and Jacey suddenly wondered what their son was like. How old was he now? If he lived in the house behind them, did he have a family? Grant and Helen hadn't mentioned any grandchildren or in-laws, and Melissa, unfortunately, had said nothing about Kale.

"Kale collected thousands of rocks." Jacey heard Grant speaking to Blaze. "He went to school and got a degree in geology."

"Really? Wow. We learned about rock layers in school, and our teacher brought a lot of rocks for us to look at. They weren't neat like these, though," Blaze replied, examining a knobby green stone. It looked like a wad of marbles melted together. "Can you find these here?"

"Sure can," Grant responded enthusiastically. "You just need to know where to look."

"This is a wonderful room," Jacey added.

"Can we see Mom's room?" Blaze asked, replacing the green rock.

Directly across the hall was another room of similar size, and Jacey couldn't help but hide a quick smile. Ceramic chickens peeked out of every nook and cranny. Pictures of roosters and bright, fluffy chickens adorned the walls. A large vase of artificial daisies filled the top of the dresser, and chickens meandered through the green stems and leaves. The bed looked soft and comfortable with its bright yellow and white bedspread and chicken-shaped pillows.

"This is Allison's room. She's attending BYU in Provo right now. She's our youngest, and she just got engaged last weekend to Tom Ernie. He's a boy that lives here in town," Helen announced proudly. "She likes—well, chickens." Helen laughed as she picked up a ceramic rooster from the dresser. She gave Jacey a crooked smile, and Jacey couldn't help but laugh.

"I love it, Aunt Helen. Honest." She grinned back, eyeing the comfy-looking bed. The billowing blankets made her yearn for its softness. She was beginning to feel the exhausting effects of the last several days.

"Well, what about a big glass of milk and a couple of cookies before bed? Then you can just rest until your heart's content. You must be so tired." Helen placed a comforting arm around Jacey's waist. "We're just so glad you're here, Melissa." She gave Jacey a quick squeeze.

"Thank you," Jacey replied quietly. She would never get used to being called Melissa.

FIVE

Jacey sighed as she crossed Blaze's room to close the blinds. She eyed herself in the darkened window for a moment before shutting the blinds against the night. She turned back toward Blaze and watched with a weary smile as her son jumped into bed. The large pine bed dwarfed his skinny frame, and she teasingly asked, "Are you going to get lost in that?"

Blaze grinned. "Yep, I've never seen such a big bed. This is a cool room, huh, Mom?"

Jacey stepped to the bed and pulled the thick quilt up to his chin. "It *is* a cool room," she had to agree.

"Hey, can I watch TV while I fall asleep?" he asked with a hopeful expression.

Jacey laughed before replying. "No."

His young face fell. "Aw, Mom."

"No," Jacey repeated firmly. "You know I don't like late-night television. You can watch cartoons in the morning."

"I can't wait to ride the horse tomorrow with my saddle and my hat." Blaze's eyes twinkled with renewed excitement. "Look how awesome it looks." He flipped onto his side and reached over to touch the white hat hanging on the bedpost next to his head.

Jacey thoughtfully fingered the stiff brim, and her heart twisted with guilt. Helen and Grant had been so loving and accepting of "Melissa" and her son. What would it do to them if

39

they discovered her ruse? The thought scared Jacey.

"I can't wait. Wait till Jenny finds out," Blaze's excited chatter broke through Jacey's troubled thoughts.

"Oh, that will be fun, won't it, Blaze?" She forced a small smile, but Blaze's excited expression quickly faded.

"They're really nice people, huh, Mom?" He watched Jacey's face closely.

"Yes, they are. I hate to deceive them," she told him truthfully.

"You mean pretend to be Melissa?" he whispered.

"Yes, that's what I mean." Jacey sighed, bending down to kiss the top of his head.

"Dad can't find us here, can he, Mom?" Blaze's eyes narrowed with concern.

"No, he can't, and one day we'll tell Uncle Grant and Aunt Helen the truth, all right?"

"I wish they were really our aunt and uncle. Jenny's lucky."

Jacey frowned. Ever since John's mother had died, Blaze hadn't had any other relatives besides herself and John. Melissa was the closest "relative" they had. The thought suddenly made Jacey terribly lonely, and her heart ached for her child. She longed to give him the family she had so desperately wanted when she'd first married John.

"I wish so too," she whispered hoarsely. She kissed him and switched off the lamp. "Now go to sleep. You can't go riding if you're too tired. You'll fall off the horse." Jacey reached through the darkness to lightly touch his face. She could feel him smile.

"No, I won't, Mom." He laughed. "Hey, I'm going to look like a real cowboy, aren't I?"

Jacey laughed at his anticipation. "You sure are, Tex."

She moved toward the door. The hallway light spilled across the front of the room, and Jacey smiled at her son. He was growing so fast.

"I'm going to take a shower. I'll leave my bedroom door open so you can come over if you need me, all right?" She blew him a quick kiss. "Good night, Blaze. I love you."

"'Night, Mom," Blaze said as he flopped toward the opposite wall. "I love you too."

• • •

Jacey exhaled slowly as hot water washed over her sore, exhausted body. It had been a worrying day. She hoped the shower would help to ease her tension before she slipped into bed. Guilt seemed to be her constant companion the last few days. She knew that if she was going to pull this stunt off, she would need to ignore the shame she felt.

I have no other choice, she reminded herself firmly. She would just have to be the best "Melissa" she could be if she was going succeed—and she had to succeed. She had to stay hidden from John. Whether or not he had murdered Sharon Ivan, Jacey knew without a doubt that once he found her, he would take Blaze. She would die before she would allow her son to be in the hands of that monster again.

"Mmm," Jacey moaned when the shower began to cool.

She reluctantly flipped off the water and stepped into the steamy interior of the small bathroom. She wrapped her body in a large, fluffy towel before stepping to the mirror, wiping at the thin layer of steam with the palm of her hand, and eyeing herself through the streaked reflection. She had to admit, she had never looked as healthy as she did now. It was strange seeing her fair complexion so clear. There were no bruises or scratches that needed to be concealed with heavy makeup or dark glasses. John hadn't abused her constantly, but the bruises he had left had always seemed to linger.

Jacey raised a hand to touch the scar that marred her forehead. It had faded over the years. It was barely noticeable anymore, but Jacey cringed as she tentatively touched the thin, white line. Blaze had been four months old at the time. He had just started teething. John had come home late again and, as always, he'd been in a foul mood.

• • •

She did her best to calm Blaze through dinner, knowing John hated to hear the baby fuss.

"Will you shut him up, Jacey?" he demanded angrily as he pushed his half-eaten dinner away.

41

"He's cutting teeth—I don't know what to do to help him," Jacey said quietly.

"You never know what to do, do you, Jacey?" he replied before he stomped upstairs, leaving Jacey alone with Blaze.

An hour later, Jacey had finally calmed Blaze, and he had fallen asleep. Although she was exhausted, Jacey had returned to the kitchen to wash up after dinner. She cleared the table and filled the sink with hot, soapy water. There were a lot of dishes, and Jacey knew she would be washing for at least an hour. They had a dishwasher, but John wouldn't let her use it. He preferred the dishes to be washed and dried by hand, and the metal pans always needed to be polished and shined before she could place them on the rack above the bar.

As she finished the dishes, she heard John descending the stairs. She glanced toward him to give him a quick smile before turning back to place a stack of plates in the cupboard above the sink. He came up behind her and placed his arms gently around her waist.

"Baby asleep?" he asked as he nuzzled her neck.

Jacey nodded, then groaned quietly when he moved up to her ear. She was so exhausted. "Not now, John," she pleaded. "I'm tired."

Immediately, Jacey knew she'd made a mistake. John's arms tightened and she felt his sharp, indrawn breath. Suddenly, his hand cupped the back of her head, and he slammed her forehead against the cupboard. Blinding light engulfed Jacey, and she fell back against the hard, tiled floor. Through the haze she heard John's heavy receding footsteps. The front door opened and slammed shut.

Stunned, Jacey lay on the floor. She felt dizzy, and blood clouded her vision. Through the distance she heard Blaze crying. Sick with pain, she crawled across the kitchen to reach a towel to place against the gash on her head. Blaze's cries were growing louder, causing Jacey's vision to spin. Her stomach turned violently, and she threw up.

Somehow, she made it into the nursery and fell asleep with Blaze in her arms. The next morning she woke up with a throbbing headache. The gash across her forehead was swollen and crusted with dried blood and she knew she'd have to hide the dark circles under her eyes.

That afternoon, John called to say he was sorry. He sent roses and a new dress (which she hated). That evening after he came home, he took her in his arms, held her gently, kissed her, and promised he would never *hurt her again. She believed him then. She always desperately wanted to believe him.*

• • •

Jacey breathed deeply, trying to shake the memory. She would never let another man hurt her again, and John would never take her son. John always warned her that if she left, he would take Blaze, but she would never let that happen.

"Not ever," she whispered into the silence.

Jacey sighed wearily as she ran a comb through her wet, tangled hair and then turned down her bed covers. The sheets felt cool and crisp, and Jacey relished the feel of the firm bed. She closed her eyes, and exhaustion won as she quickly fell into a deep sleep.

• • •

"Don't you have anything better to do?" Ronald snarled.

Agent Parker grinned lazily before he turned back to his paper. "Absolutely not," he replied as he shuffled the pages of the thick *Detroit Times*. He flipped to the sports section, then groaned, "Aw, man. The Packers lost again."

Ronald blew out a long, slow breath and moved to his desk just as the phone began to ring. He reached for it. "This is Ronald."

Parker set the paper aside and glanced at his partner with bored curiosity. *Man, I wish this case would pick up a little*, he thought jadedly. He was bored stiff and tired of dealing with Ronald and his crotchety attitude. He usually found a great deal of pleasure in goading the older man, but even that was becoming tiresome. Parker sighed and reached for his paper again, for lack of anything else to do, just as Ronald's angry "What?!" bounced across the small office.

The older man's face twisted with irritation as he yelled into the phone, "What do you mean 'she's gone'? How on earth did you two lose her?"

Agent Parker smirked, then stood as Ronald continued to growl into the phone. "How long has she been gone?" he asked. After a short pause. "Well, find her!" he barked before slamming the phone down.

Parker winced. He watched his agitated partner with interest as a slight smile played at the corner of his lips. Ronald groaned and ran a hand through his ever-thinning hair.

"What's up?" Parker asked. "They lost her?"

"They've been tagging her back and forth to work for the last few days. They said she was driving toward the kid's school when they lost her. She never showed at the café, and when they went back to check the school, the kid had never shown up." Ronald sighed and rubbed the back of his neck. "That woman knows something or she wouldn't have run!"

"Well, then." Parker grinned in anticipation. It would be good to have a bit more stimulation. "Looks like we've got some work do to, Chief."

"You think?" Ronald put in sarcastically, his frown intensifying. "Come on. Let's get out of here."

"Great." Parker threw the newspaper down onto the chair. "I needed a bit more excitement today. I was getting tired of staring at the back of your head already."

• • •

Jacey woke feeling disoriented and confused. Light streamed through the thin lace curtains and fanned across the foot of her bed. She sat up quickly; the clock read seven-thirty. Jacey couldn't believe she had slept so late. Her usual schedule would have had her up at five. Throwing the covers back, she rose from the bed. Padding across the hallway in her bare feet, Jacey entered Blaze's room. Surprised to find him still snuggled deep into the thick comforter, she stepped back toward her own room. Normally, Blaze would have been awake and anxious to watch Saturday morning cartoons, but the drive had been tiring, and she was glad that Blaze could rest.

Once in her room, Jacey quietly shut the door so that she could dress. Lifting her heavy cases, she dropped them on the bed and searched for an outfit. Feeling anxious for the day ahead, Jacey decided she needed to dress comfortably. She pulled a pair of old jeans and the T-shirt she had purchased at a gas station in Nebraska from her stuffed cases and quickly dressed. She groaned as she tugged on her Levis. They were getting tighter, and if she wasn't careful she would end up on one of those terrible "women" diets too.

Smiling to herself, she stepped to the large mirror that sat above the dresser. The summer sun had brought out several freckles across the bridge of her nose and cheek line. She would have to remember to buy some sunscreen when she got a chance to go into town.

Jacey pulled her thick hair into a loose ponytail, applied a touch of mascara and eye shadow, then turned to look out the window at the yard below. The large back lawn was thick and recently mowed. A giant cottonwood tree bordered the edge of the grass, shading a redwood picnic table under its thick foliage. A haphazard fence made of wood and thick wire separated the yard from the pastures that stretched on behind the house.

The new grass in the open fields shone bright against the morning sun. Squatty trees grew sparsely across the fields and more abundantly as they neared the hills beyond. A large, newer house sat in a clearing among the trees, just at the base of a hill. *That must be Kale's house*, Jacey thought fleetingly. There were cattle further out, and three horses grazed serenely in the fields closest to the house. The view was breathtaking—like a painting.

"Hey, Mom!"

Jacey jumped when Blaze suddenly burst through her bedroom door. She turned from the window to face her smiling son. Dressed in jeans, an old T-shirt, and already wearing his hat, he looked ready to face the day.

"Good, you're ready. Let's go down." Blaze reached for her hand.

"Well, good morning to you too." She couldn't help but laugh at her son's enthusiasm.

"Come on," Blaze insisted.

"Well, good morning," Helen said, looking up from a sink full of dishes as Jacey and Blaze stepped down into the dining room.

"Good morning," Jacey replied, feeling awkward. She could smell the tantalizing aroma of a freshly cooked breakfast.

Blaze moved into the kitchen, and Helen turned toward him, drying her hands with a towel. "You look very handsome," she commented.

"Is Uncle Grant already outside?" Blaze asked impatiently.

Helen laughed at the boy's obvious excitement. "He sure is. Uncle Grant and Kale have been up for hours already."

"Really?" Blaze asked bewildered.

"When you live on a farm, you have to be up before the sun. We have cows and horses and chickens to feed. The stalls have to be mucked and cleaned, and new hay has to be put down. It takes a lot of work to run a farm," Helen said.

"It's like a real farm! Can I help?" Blaze asked with growing excitement.

Helen smiled. "You most certainly can, but not until you've eaten one of my homemade farm breakfasts."

Blaze's face fell slightly, but he recovered with a quick smile when Helen turned to pull a bowl of fresh strawberries and a plate of thick, steaming waffles off the counter.

"Oh, you didn't need to cook breakfast for us. I hate to put you through any trouble," Jacey put in quickly.

"Nonsense." Helen ushered Jacey and Blaze toward the table. "I have fresh eggs and bacon staying warm in the microwave."

Jacey paused next to the table. "Can I help with anything?" she asked, then sat down as Helen shook her head. Blaze sat next to Jacey and eyed the back door anxiously.

"Can I just go help Uncle Grant?" he asked. Jacey eyed him firmly, feeling slightly embarrassed.

"Blaze, you need to eat some breakfast first," she told him quietly as Helen brought a heaping plate of bacon and eggs to the table.

"Oh, land sakes, they'll have plenty of work left for you to help with. I know Uncle Grant could use your help with the horses this morning," said Helen.

"Really?" Blaze's expression brightened.

"Now, these eggs are some of our very own," Helen informed them proudly. "Nothing tastes better than fresh eggs."

"This looks wonderful, Aunt Helen." Jacey filled her plate

with food. It had been ages since she'd had a real, homemade breakfast. She hadn't cooked breakfast since before her divorce. "We don't usually get a chance for a real breakfast. We usually just manage with dry cereal and coffee."

"Oh—oh dear."

Jacey looked up as Helen spoke. Aunt Helen's face looked stricken.

"What is it?" Jacey asked. Her eyes broadened in concern.

"I'm afraid I forgot all about coffee. You see, when Grant and I joined the LDS church, we stopped drinking it. I—well, I didn't even think to have any on hand. I am so sorry," Helen hurriedly explained.

"Oh," Jacey began, not quite sure she understood. "You mean, when you joined the Mormon Church?" she asked.

"Yes. You see, the Mormon Church is The Church of Jesus Christ of Latter-Day Saints. As you can see," Helen laughed, "that can be a mouthful. So, many members refer to our church as the LDS church."

"I see." Jacey nodded her understanding. "So . . . Mormons don't drink coffee?" She felt slightly embarrassed for asking.

"No. Most choose not to," Helen replied with a smile. "We don't drink alcohol, coffee, or tea. It's part of the Word of Wisdom. It's sort of like a—well, a health guideline for our church," Helen explained.

Jacey nodded slowly. "Oh, well, please don't worry about coffee. I usually just drink it when Mel—" She stopped suddenly. "I mean, I usually only drink it when I'm at work. I really don't need it, and I wouldn't want you to buy it on my behalf." She had almost told Helen that she only drank it on the mornings when Melissa had gotten up to make it. She was going to have to be more careful or she would blow it fast.

"Can we go ride the horses this morning?" Blaze asked just as he stuffed a bite of waffle in his mouth.

"Blaze, slow down before you choke," Jacey quickly admonished, although she was grateful for the turn in conversation.

"I bet Uncle Grant has—" Helen began just as the washroom door thumped open and Grant's large frame filled the kitchen.

"Well, good morning, beautiful ladies," Grant said boisterously. His faded coveralls were caked with dry mud and a wilted, wide-brimmed hat sat on his head. "Looks like you're ready to get to work, son," he directed at Blaze with a wide grin. Jacey couldn't help but smile; he looked every bit the old farmer.

"Would you just look at that mess you left on my clean kitchen floor?" Helen suddenly jumped up from the table, and Grant looked down sheepishly at his mud-crusted boots.

Helen brushed past him to retrieve the broom from the washroom. "I just cleaned it." She poked him with the end of the broom, and Jacey couldn't help but look on as Grant grinned, wrapped his arms tightly about Helen's ample waist, and kissed her soundly.

"Give me that," he grunted and pulled the broom from Helen's grasp. "I'll clean it right up." He laughed good-naturedly, and Jacey looked down at her plate.

The scene with Grant and Helen left her unexpectedly shaken. She forced her attention back to her breakfast as an unbidden memory crowded her mind. She had been seven months pregnant, and she'd spent the day cleaning and scrubbing their large house, as John always expected the house to be spotless. It had rained all day, and he tracked mud onto the clean living room floor. Jacey had snapped at him, and he'd smacked her for the first time, telling her to "mind herself" and reminding her that it was "his house," and her job was to clean it. He had come in later that night and apologized. He said he'd had a bad day at work, and he'd promised to never hit her again.

Jacey sighed. She tried to focus on eating, but suddenly she didn't feel very hungry.

"Well?" Grant replaced the broom and dust pan, then turned to face Blaze, "You ready, boy?"

"Uh-huh." Blaze nodded, swallowing his last bite of waffle.

"Come on, then." Grant beckoned Blaze with a wave of his hand, then turned to Jacey, "That is, if it's all right with you, Mom?"

Blaze turned expectant eyes toward her, and she forced a quick smile. It was good to see her son's enthusiasm. "Go on," she told him as he jumped up from the table. "You mind Uncle Grant," she reminded him when he stepped past the large man and moved toward the back door.

"I will, Mom," he called.

"He'll be fine." Grant winked before he turned to follow Blaze. Jacey could hear the creaking of the screen door and a loud bang as it shut behind them.

"Every little boy longs for open spaces," Helen commented, turning back toward Jacey.

"I haven't seen him this excited in a long time. This will be a great experience for him." Jacey stood to help clear their breakfast dishes.

"Grant's been so excited to teach him how to ride. It's been a long while since we had a young boy around. It seems like our kids grew up so fast." Helen sighed as she picked up an empty bowl.

"You just have the two?" Jacey hoped her question wouldn't raise any suspicions. Melissa hadn't mentioned cousins.

Helen nodded. "Kale will turn thirty-two next month, and Allison—my goodness—getting married." Helen shook her head and smiled reflectively. "They're good kids. Kale owns a good portion of the land east of here, but he always helps Grant. He's a good man."

Jacey moved into the kitchen with a small stack of dishes. She put them in the sink just as Helen came up behind her and placed a bowl on top of the small stack.

"Can I do these dishes?" Jacey asked, turning on the hot water.

"Oh no, you don't." Helen nudged Jacey out of the way with a grin. "You're on vacation. Besides, there are only a few. It'll take only a moment to wash these up."

"I don't mind." Jacey laughed quietly as Helen shook her head again.

"Land sakes, no. You go on out and enjoy the morning before it gets too hot."

"Well, thank you for breakfast. It was delicious," Jacey replied sincerely. She stepped into the cluttered washroom and then out into the Jackman's back yard.

Somewhere in the distance, she could hear a dog barking and the sound of a bee buzzing past. The air felt crisp and refreshing. Shading her eyes from the sun, Jacey gazed out across the pasture. She could make out a rider on a horse, back by the trees, and a large dog bounding alongside in the tall grass. She fleetingly wondered if that was Kale before her attention turned to the sound of Blaze and Grant's muffled voices a little ways off. She could hear Grant's deep voice and Blaze's shrill laughter.

Jacey was surprised that Blaze had taken to Grant so quickly. Usually he was very cautious around men, but she was glad Grant had taken him under his wing and that Blaze was responding so well. He needed this. It would be nice for her son to have a good male role model, if only for a short time. She knew that Blaze had seen far too much of John's abusive behavior and angry temperament.

She heard Blaze laugh again. Curious, she moved in the direction of the corrals. As she stepped around the tree, she could see Blaze standing on the railings of an enclosed corral. Blaze moved up another rail and extended his hand toward a young horse standing in the middle.

"Slowly now." She heard Grant's soft-spoken directions.

Jacey stopped and held her breath as the young colt inched cautiously closer to Blaze's outstretched hand. Her son grinned as the horse drew near and took the small carrot Blaze held for him.

"Good job!" Grant grinned, slapping Blaze on the back.

Blaze turned, suddenly seeing Jacey. He jumped down and raced toward her. "Did you see that? Did you see me, Mom?"

Jacey smiled. "You did so well, Blaze." She hugged him tightly.

"Guess what?" Blaze spoke breathlessly, "Uncle Grant says that's *my* horse."

Jacey glanced up toward the horse. Its deep brown coat shone brilliantly in the morning light.

"I can even name him," Blaze continued.

Jacey studied the horse with interest. It had a white star-like patch on its forehead and one white hoof. It was a beautiful animal. "That's so exciting, Blaze, but—" Jacey stopped herself and smiled at her son's lively face. He turned back toward the corral, and Jacey glanced on nervously. *Grant can't really mean to give Blaze that horse*, she thought, surprised.

"Come and see him, Mom," Blaze called to Jacey as she approached the corral. She caught Grant's eye, and he winked as Blaze continued. "Isn't he so cool, Mom? Uncle Grant says I have to learn how to feed him and saddle him before we can go riding. Then, after that, I have to brush him down with a big hairbrush. Uncle Grant says he needs to get to know me. And see? He likes me already, because he ate out of my hand," he finished eagerly.

"That's wonderful, Blaze." Jacey laughed as she stepped next to the corral.

Grant turned into the small tack shed and quickly returned, carrying Blaze's saddle and a thick, wool blanket.

"So, have you come up with a name for that colt yet?" Grant asked.

Blaze eyed his horse carefully before answering, "No, not yet, I have to think more. It's got to be a good one. Hey, Mom." Blaze turned excited eyes toward Jacey. "You want to feed him?" he asked.

Jacey hesitated for a short moment before she nodded with a little smile. "Sure, I guess I could try."

"I'll be back. I got to go get another carrot." Blaze turned and dashed toward the house.

Grant laughed, and Jacey quickly added, "Thank you. This means so much to him."

Grant turned away from the saddle. He'd been working on adjusting a couple of straps. "Every boy needs a good horse," he told her with a grin.

Jacey paused thoughtfully before she asked, "You didn't really give him the horse, did you?" She suddenly felt foolish for asking.

"Sure did." Grant stepped closer. Placing his large hand on Jacey's thin shoulder, he went on, "It's his for as long as you stay, and it's his as often as you come. And I hope you stay long and come often, Melissa."

Jacey shuffled her feet, suddenly feeling very uncomfortable.

"You know," Grant continued. Jacey shyly met his eyes. "A

man needs his family, and I've been terrible lonesome for mine." He inhaled loudly and turned to look out across the field.

Jacey stepped back a little. "Oh, I—" she stopped, unsure of what to say, but was saved from having to say anything when Grant spoke again.

"You know your dad and I, we used to dream of working a ranch together. He and I weren't always at odds with one another. No, he was my best friend, and I loved him. I wish I'd had the chance to tell him that before he died." Grant's voice suddenly grew husky with emotion, and Jacey couldn't help the tears that suddenly burned the back of her eyes. Guilt washed over her in waves as she watched Grant's haunted eyes.

"I'm sorry," she whispered. She was sorry. It must have been hard for him to lose his brother. She was sorry she couldn't be more comfort to him, and she suddenly felt very sorry she wasn't Melissa. Grant turned to face her once again, and Jacey met his kind eyes.

"As someone once said, 'it is better to lose your pride with someone you love than to lose that someone you love with your useless pride.'" He cleared the emotion from his throat. "Oh well. Water under the bridge. You're here now, and that's enough." He suddenly pulled her into a tight embrace.

Startled, Jacey placed her arms around the older man. His thick arms released her just as Blaze came tearing back across the yard.

"I got one, Mom," he called.

She took the carrot from Blaze's outstretched hand, grateful for the interruption, yet feeling strangely sorry that the moment was gone. Grant and Helen were everything she had dreamed of in a family, and she was rapidly falling in love with the thought of belonging to them. This deception was more than she had bargained for. She and Blaze would need to leave sooner than she'd planned. They had to.

"All right." Jacey forced her mind toward the horse. "Tell me how to do this," she directed at Blaze.

• • •

Jacey watched with pride when Blaze tightened his saddle straps, just as Uncle Grant had shown him.

"That's it, son. Now remember, it's always safe to check the saddle once in a while during the ride."

"Kay," Blaze said before he turned to give Jacey a fleeting smile.

"You ready to ride him?" Grant asked, and Blaze nodded eagerly.

Jacey held her breath when Grant showed Blaze how to mount his horse. He gave the boy a boost, and Blaze's eyes widened apprehensively as he placed his feet in the stirrups. The horse took a few steps, and Grant quickly reached out to steady the animal.

"Okay now?" Grant asked Blaze.

"Uh-huh."

"You just hang on tight. I'll lead him around a couple times so you can get used to the feel of him. Then we'll head out across them fields, all right?" Grant took the horse's bit and gave a gentle tug.

Jacey smiled and then laughed as Blaze risked a quick wave in her direction. "You're doing so well," she called out to him.

"Bye, Mom," Blaze replied, and Jacey watched as Grant opened the gate on the opposite side, leading to the pasture.

"Be careful," Jacey called back.

Grant gave a quick wave. "He'll be fine. He's doing great." He led the horse through the opening.

Jacey watched as Blaze, using the reins, led the horse at a slow walk through the tall grass. With a deep sigh, she turned to find a place to sit. A worn wooden bench near the tack shed looked inviting, and Jacey sat down gingerly, being careful to avoid slivers. She could smell the thick scent of leather and earth, and she breathed in, enjoying the unique mix of smells.

Leaning back against the sun-baked wall of the shed, she reveled in the warmth. A slight breeze brushed across her face, and she couldn't help but notice how quiet it seemed. She could barely make out the faint grumble of cars in the distance. How different everything was from the lives she and Blaze led. Jacey wondered fleetingly what things could have been like for her if she had only made a few different decisions in her early years.

What was it like to be married to man like Grant Jackman? He seemed sincere and truly kind. Helen wasn't afraid of him. They laughed and joked and grumbled at one another with love. Love was something Jacey had been searching for since her parents' accident, but she'd gone looking for it in all the wrong places.

She smiled slightly when she caught sight of Blaze in the distance. Grant's tall form led the colt vigilantly. She brushed back a few stray hairs that danced in the breeze, then stood and stretched. The sun was making her feel lazy. She let her gaze wander around the yard, taking in her surroundings. The place smelt strongly of hay and dirt and, she guessed, horses. She smiled. The tangy, unpleasant smell definitely had to be horses.

Feeling an urge to explore, Jacey stepped around the small tack shed and headed across the yard toward what she could only guess was the barn. It looked nothing like the big red barns she had always associated with a farm; rather, it was large and made out of aluminum siding. Its shape was similar to that of a barn, but it was green and white.

She approached the large barn, feeling a bit apprehensive. She wondered if Grant minded her exploring inside. She had never been inside a barn before, and curiosity won out when she heard the unmistakable whinny of a horse coming from inside. She stepped through the large door and stood still as her eyes adjusted from the brightness of the day to the barn's dim light.

The smell of hay and horses was a bit overpowering, but she gazed across the length of the building, intrigued. Several green-painted, metal stalls sat along the north end of the building, while the opposite side was stacked high with clean bales of straw, tied tightly with bright orange and brown twine. She heard a quiet snort, and she took a tentative step forward before she saw a horse's black head move in a stall further back.

After making sure the animal was secured in its stall, Jacey moved closer. The horse was larger than she had first suspected, and its beautiful black coat shone brilliantly. Jacey could see how strong the animal was as the muscles in its forelegs quivered. The horse shook its magnificent head and pawed the ground as if it ached to run.

"Hi," Jacey spoke softly, approaching the stall with caution.

The horse moved toward her, stretching its head over the tall, green slats. Jacey timidly put her hand forward to touch the animal's smooth nose. The horse seemed friendly. Encouraged, Jacey moved closer to rub its thick neck just as she had seen Grant do with the colt.

The horse bumped Jacey gently with its muzzle, and Jacey couldn't help but laugh aloud. "Hi to you too. You're a friendly girl."

The horse nudged her again. Its hot breath blew across her face and bare arms. She brought her face closer, feeling excited and nervous. She had never been so close to such a large animal before, and she couldn't help but enjoy the new experience. The horse nudged her once again, and Jacey laughed cheerfully.

"What do you want, girl?" Jacey smiled into the animal's large black eyes. "What's your name? What is it, girl?" she asked quietly.

"*His* name is Athabasca's Gold, and he's probably looking for food."

Startled, Jacey turned in the direction of the barn door. Her heart hammered against her ribs as she watched a large man move away from the door and walk toward her. Jacey caught her breath and brought a hand to her beating chest. He had scared her. She hadn't heard him approach. His eyes held hers as he moved toward her, and Jacey instinctively took a step away from the stall when he came and placed a large tanned hand against the horse's neck.

"You must be Kale," Jacey said, feeling self-conscious. She smiled before she realized he was openly glaring at her.

"And you are Melissa?" he spoke gruffly, and Jacey nodded mutely.

He removed his hand from the horse, then brushed past her to retrieve a bucket from the opposite side of the barn. He stepped back toward her, eyeing her frankly. Jacey squirmed under his open scrutiny. She lifted her chin, and his eyes narrowed. He turned back toward the horse. He brought the bucket forward, and the horse eagerly dipped its nose in.

"There you go, boy," Kale's voice softened as he patted the side of the horse's neck, and Jacey watched the man continue to speak in subdued tones to the horse.

He was tall, much taller than Grant, and built thick through his chest and arms. Jacey guessed his height was about six-two or so. He was wearing dusty coveralls similar to those Grant had been wearing. His boots were caked with mud, and deep brown hair stuck out from underneath a dusty, blue baseball cap that read BYU on the front. Jacey caught a hint of dark stubble on his scowling face.

"He's a beautiful horse," Jacey commented when it became apparent Kale wasn't going to say anything to her.

He turned cold eyes toward her, and Jacey knew immediately that this man did not like her. Had she been wrong to come in the barn?

"He is," he spoke abruptly and stepped past her once again to retrieve a metal brush from a small table that sat against the back wall. He said nothing else, and Jacey cleared her throat in the uncomfortable silence.

"I hope it was okay that I came in here. I just thought—"

"I don't care that you came in here. This isn't my barn," Kale spoke brusquely, making it ever more apparent that he did not want her around.

Confused by his uncouth behavior, Jacey spoke curtly, "Well, it was good to finally meet you, Kale."

She turned toward the door. Kale said nothing as she stepped outside into the blinding light of the early afternoon. She paused a moment while her eyes adjusted to the change. The man was ill-mannered beyond belief, and Jacey shuddered at being treated so rudely. She hadn't known the man long enough for him to treat her in such a way. Jacey frowned at the thought and turned toward the house. What had she done to deserve this man's resentment? She definitely did not like Kale.

SIX

"The beautiful Ms. Gold said Jacey Grayson pulled the kid out of school the day before Johnston lost them. Grayson told the school that she found a new job out in Kalamazoo," Parker announced as he approached Agent Ronald outside the main doors of the elementary school.

"Kalamazoo?" Ronald grunted. "Kalamazoo is a good three hours from here, and that's not including traffic."

"Yeah. Hey, a buddy of mine went to college out there—Western Michigan University. He got a degree in psychology." Parker grinned.

"Really?" Ronald scowled. "Well, I don't suppose your buddy could help us find Jacey Grayson?" he added sarcastically.

"Doubt it. So what's next?"

Ronald shook his head and glowered at the busy street in front of the school. "Call Johnston—get him and his partner headed down to Kalamazoo. Tell him to scour that city until he finds her."

"Aw, Chief. I was looking forward to a road trip." Parker laughed just as his cell phone rang. He flipped open the phone. "Parker here."

Ronald tapped his foot impatiently as he listened to Agent Parker's one-sided conversation. This case was becoming more complicated by the minute. He didn't believe for a second that Jacey Grayson had suddenly decided to move clear across the state.

"Hey, Chief."

Ronald heard Parker's phone flip shut, and he turned to face the younger agent. "Yeah?"

"That was the SAC in the Chicago office. A couple of agents tracking John Trent say he caught a jet our way. It looks like we're not the only ones looking for Jacey Grayson."

"That's great." Ronald groaned loudly. "That's just great. Did they say where Trent was?"

"No—see, that's the bad news." Parker grimaced. "They lost track of Trent once he hit Wayne County."

Ronald sighed. "Well, let's get to it. We'd better move fast," he replied before moving down the stairs toward their vehicle.

• • •

Jacey relished the taste of her warm, buttered muffin as she sat in Helen's cozy kitchen. She had never tasted muffins made from scratch. She was afraid that between the cookies, bread, and other treats Helen was preparing, she would be waddling by the time she and Blaze left. Pushing down her sudden guilt, Jacey swallowed the last bite and reached for another.

"These are heaven," Jacey commented between mouthfuls.

"I'm glad you like them. I invited Kale over to have some, but he said he's too busy with the farm and his paperwork. He's got another business trip next week. I'm so sorry you haven't had a chance to meet him yet." Helen bent down to place a pan in the oven.

"Oh, I met him," Jacey replied. "He found me exploring the barn." She tried to keep her tone neutral, but as far as she was concerned, Kale was an arrogant, mannerless brute. Jacey wasn't sure what she had expected, but she certainly hadn't been prepared for the way he'd treated her and she was, more than ever, determined not to let another man intimidate her again.

"Well, that's fantastic," Helen replied cheerfully.

"Can I help with anything?" Jacey asked, hoping to change the subject. "I'm not much of a cook, but if you show me how, I'd love to learn."

Helen smiled. "Well, if you want to, I suppose I could use the help. Have you ever made bread?"

Jacey shook her head.

"Well then, I'm going to teach you. Nothing tastes better than home-baked bread." Helen smiled, turning into the pantry to pull out another sack of flour.

Jacey joined her in the kitchen. "I have to admit, I've never baked anything that didn't originate from a box."

"Oh dear," Helen breathed.

Jacey laughed.

"Well, I always try to finish up all my baking before Sunday, so now is as good a time as any for you to learn." Helen instructed Jacey on how to mix ingredients and the proper way to knead the dough. She and Helen were laughing at one of Helen's baking fiasco stories when Blaze suddenly burst through the door.

"Wow, Mom! You should have seen me," he called excitedly, kicking off his muddy shoes in the washroom. He padded into the kitchen with stocking feet.

Jacey wiped the flour off her hands. "Well," she grinned, "tell me all about it."

"I raced Uncle Grant's horse, and I did it all by myself too. Uncle Grant didn't hold the horse. I did it alone. And me and Ocotillo won."

"Really? And who is Oco—who?" she asked.

Blaze grinned. The sun had brought out a thick spattering of freckles on his face, and a streak of dirt covered one cheek. He looked like a boy his age should, and Jacey's heart swelled with pride.

"It's Oh—ko—TEE—oh," he pronounced slowly, "Ocotillo."

"Is that what you named your horse?" Jacey asked, surprised by the unusual name.

"Uh-huh. Great, isn't it?" he said as he spied the muffins. "Can I have one of those, Mom?" he asked hopefully, and Helen giggled behind them.

"You certainly can," Helen told him. She pulled a small plate from the counter.

"You'd better go and wash up first," Jacey quickly reminded her son.

Once Blaze was settled at the kitchen table with clean hands and a muffin, Jacey returned to her bread.

"That's a strange name for your horse, Blaze. What does it mean?" she called over to him.

"It's a cactus," he told her between bites. "Kale—" he swallowed, "Kale showed one to me when we stopped by his house."

"You went to Kale's house, did you?" Helen asked. "I bet that was an adventure in itself," she directed at Blaze. "Kale collects all sort of weird plants and rocks," she added as an aside to Jacey. "He loves things like that."

"Yeah," Blaze spoke up importantly, "he says Indians in Arizona build houses using ocotillo and mud. Kale says they get real big, sometimes twelve feet long."

"Really?" Jacey asked as she pounded her dough. Somehow beating on a mound of dough made talk of Kale more bearable. "What do they look like?"

"Like whips with really sharp thorns," he replied with his mouth full of muffin.

"Well, that's a neat name for your horse," she told him with a forced smile.

Blaze finished his first muffin, and Helen promptly gave him a second. "Thanks. Hey, guess what?" he asked excitedly.

"What?" Jacey and Helen asked in unison.

"Kale showed me his fossils too. He's got shark teeth and shells and he knows where to find amm . . . amm . . . I don't remember what they're called." He turned to Helen with questioning eyes.

"Ammonites?" Helen suggested.

"Yeah, that's it, ammonites. They're squids from back when the dinosaurs lived."

"Wow," Jacey responded.

"Yep, and Kale said he would take me to find some."

"He did, huh?" Jacey couldn't help the note of resentment that crept into her voice. She didn't like the thought of Blaze spending any time with a man like Kale. She usually didn't trust first impressions, but she was fairly certain she would never like Kale. "Well, I'm glad that you had such a good time, babe," Jacey told him before she gave her dough another hard squeeze.

"What are you making?" Blaze asked, popping the last of his muffin into his mouth before he came over to watch.

"Bread. Aunt Helen's showing me how to make it."

"What are you doing?" he asked, watching Jacey squeeze the thick ball in her fists.

"She's kneading it. And it looks like you're about done." Helen came up behind Jacey to inspect her work. "Now we just put it in the pan and let it rise for a bit."

Helen handed a pan to Blaze, and he in turn handed it to Jacey. She placed her dough carefully in the pan, just as she had seen Helen do, then walked to the sink to wash her hands. She dried her hands before she placed her arms around Blaze to give him a quick hug.

"I'm glad you had such a good time this morning," she told him quietly.

"Mom." Embarrassed, Blaze pulled out of Jacey's hug before he said a bit shyly, "Maybe you can come with us tomorrow. Uncle Grant says he could saddle one of Kale's horses for you."

Jacey nodded slightly. *Great, just what I want to do—ride one of Kale's horses*, she thought.

• • •

The rest of the day was spent in lazy conversations and more baking. Helen and Jacey made five loaves of bread, four batches of cookies, and another batch of muffins. Jacey also helped Helen with dinner. They made a chicken casserole, homemade rolls, fresh snap peas, and an apple pie. The meal was a delectable feast.

Blaze spent the day shadowing Grant and helping out with chores. He collected eggs and helped muck stalls. Then he helped Uncle Grant shoe a horse and played under the large cottonwood tree while Grant mowed the lawn. The day was filled with new experiences for both Jacey and Blaze, and by the time dinner was over, Jacey felt satisfied with the things they had learned and accomplished. She had never baked so much in the whole of her life. She thought she would be exhausted, but she felt exhilarated when she pulled her perfectly shaped bread from Helen's oven.

Helen praised her efforts with warmth and affection, and Jacey couldn't help but feel proud of her accomplishment as they sat around finishing the meal she and Helen had prepared.

"Good food," Grant groaned, placing a hand on his rounded stomach. "Too good." He groaned again and winked.

"Can I have another piece of pie?" Blaze asked, and Jacey had to smile.

Blaze had thoroughly enjoyed the meal. A homemade meal was such a novelty for them. Their meals together had usually consisted of frozen pizzas and boxed mixes, or, Jacey grimaced, fast food. Her work schedule didn't allow her much time to cook, and she wondered briefly if she would have more time once she found work in Salt Lake. She quickly pushed the thought to the back of her mind. The evening was too nice to cloud with feelings of guilt.

"You make delicious bread, Melissa," Grant commented, and Jacey smiled slightly.

"Helen's a good teacher," she said quietly.

"Nonsense, I only told you how it's done. The real talent is in how it turns out, and I'd say you've got some real talent," Helen encouraged with a warm smile.

Jacey laughed quietly, feeling a bit awkward about their praise.

"Well," Grant pushed back from the table, "I thank you ladies for the fine meal." He reached over and pulled Helen in for a quick kiss before he spoke to Jacey. "I've got to pick up a few tools from over at Kale's place. Why don't you ride over with me, Melissa?"

Jacey opened her mouth to refuse, but he went on quickly, "We'll take the Jeep. That way I can give you the grand tour before dark. Kale's got some beautiful animals back there. What do you say?" His eyes twinkled expectantly.

"Oh . . . well," Jacey began. How was she going to get out of this? She had no desire to see Kale again. "I should probably stick around and help Aunt Helen clean up dinner," she said.

Helen shook her head. "Heavens no, don't be silly. It won't take me more than a minute to have this mess cleaned up. You've helped me in that stuffy kitchen all day. Now go on and spend some time together. Besides, Uncle Grant has hogged Blaze all day. I'd say it's about my turn." Helen turned toward Blaze, and Blaze smiled shyly, his mouth still full of apple pie. "How would like to help me decorate some of those cookies?" she asked him with a hopeful smile.

Blaze swallowed quickly. "Uh-huh. That would be fun."

"All right?" Grant turned toward Jacey.

She felt cornered. "Okay," she relented.

"Great, I'll get my keys and meet you by the barn." He nodded, turning toward the washroom.

• • •

Jacey eyed the open expanse of fields as she and Grant bounced along in his battered Jeep Cherokee. Cattle were scattered here and there in the open areas, and pinion pines grew thicker as they neared the hill where Kale's large house sat, nestled between the short, stubby trees.

"Do you own all this?" she asked, amazed at the wide expanse of open land.

"Oh, no. Do you see that fence, there in the distance?" he asked. Jacey squinted in the direction he pointed. She could barely make out a fence across the stretch of pasture, but she nodded. "Our land ends there. On that side, that fence closest to us, is where it begins."

"I see," she commented as they neared Kale's large house.

Grant pulled the Jeep into the gravel drive. The thick tires crunched loudly against the small pebbles as they came to a stop, and Jacey eyed the house with hesitant interest. It was much larger than Grant and Helen's modest home. It stood two stories high with a thick brick base. New cream siding led up to a thick shingled roof and a large rock chimney. There was no lawn surrounding the house; rather, Kale had let Mother Nature do his landscaping.

Ancient, twisted cedar trees and large boulders spread across the yard. Fragrant sage brush grew among the trees, and a path made of several flat stones led to the porch. To the left side of the house was an antique tractor, and an old farm wagon sat closer toward the circular drive. Jacey had never seen a place quite like it. It was unique, and yet despite the newness of the house, the rugged yard seemed to flow well with Kale's home. The house fit the area.

"Coming?" Grant called, opening his door.

She moved to follow and when she stepped from the Jeep, she caught sight of Kale coming around the back of the house. He looked up, and an obvious frown marred his attractive features when he caught sight of her. Grant stepped around the vehicle toward her, and Kale approached them at a lazy pace. He pulled the thick, leather work gloves he had been wearing from his hands, then stuffed them into his back pocket.

"Hi, Pops," he greeted with a wry smile. He did not acknowledge Jacey, and she could once again feel her temper rise.

"Hi, son. Melissa and I thought we'd stop by. I wanted to show her the rest of the place."

"Great," Kale's voice remained monotone, and his eyes never glanced her way.

"Oh, and I came to borrow a couple of wrenches. I seemed to have misplaced my set. That bailer's giving me problems again."

"That's fine." Kale turned and headed across his yard toward a small red barn. It was set back against the base of the large hill. Grant followed and indicated that Jacey should come along.

The structure looked like the typical barn Jacey was familiar with, though it was smaller in size. Kale led them through the open doors. It smelt of hay and earth and the distinct tangy aroma of horses, similar to Uncle Grant's barn. Kale moved on toward the end of the building while Grant stopped near a stall and Jacey joined him. A stately brown horse with a long black mane stood further back against the wall. Grant extended his hand, and the animal came forward without delay. Jacey stood close to Grant and watched the animal with wonder.

"It's beautiful," she breathed and tentatively reached out to caress the horse's satin neck.

Kale approached, carrying a black tool case. He handed it to Grant before Grant proudly added, "Kale raises good stock, there's no doubt about it. Arabians are good horses. They're naturally affectionate and a good, strong breed." Kale's lips quirked slightly, and Grant added, "How's his leg?"

Kale stepped closer, leaning his muscular forearms on the top rail of the stall. He was close enough that Jacey could smell the slight scent of his lingering aftershave. "Healing faster than

I expected." He reached out and patted the horse. The animal nudged his hand playfully.

"That's good to hear," Grant commented.

"What happened to his leg?" Jacey asked, looking at Grant. She didn't want Kale to think she was speaking to him.

Grant glanced at Kale, and Kale spoke as if bored, "He tangled his leg in a roll of wire last week. It cut him up real bad."

Jacey glanced through the slats in the stall. The animal's left hind leg was bandaged with yellow wrappings.

"That's terrible," she spoke quietly. "What's his name?" She was suddenly curious.

Kale eyed her for one small moment before he added curtly, "Innoko, and he'll be fine in a few days." Then he turned his attention back to Grant. "Southern Red should be dropping her foal any day now. I might need your help." He crossed the barn toward another stall, and Grant and Jacey followed in turn.

They stepped across the hay-strewn floor, and Jacey commented, "Your horses have such unique names."

"That's because my horses are unique," he told her shortly.

Jacey scowled behind his back.

Kale stepped up to another stall where a very round, very pregnant horse stood. The horse greeted Kale with a wave of her head, and Kale patted her gently.

"Kale names most of his animals after the places he's visited in Alaska or the Middle East," Grant explained. He smiled with embarrassment.

"I see," Jacey responded quietly. "She looks different from the others." She noticed the horse's unique build and coloring. Southern Red seemed to be larger and stockier than the other horses that Jacey had seen on the ranch so far. Jacey studied the horse carefully. Her chestnut coat shone brilliantly with copper highlights. The horse's mane and tail were light, and she had a single white spot on her right hip.

"Most of Kale's stock are Arabians," Grant clarified when it became apparent Kale wouldn't. "But Red here, she's a trail horse. They're gentle creatures, and they go almost anywhere you point them."

Jacey reached up to rub the mare's nose. The horse jerked slightly, and Grant laughed when Jacey jumped.

"Oh, she don't mind you, none. She's just been a bit touchy lately."

Jacey glanced back into the animal's immense eyes. She could see her reflection mirrored in the black depths of the horse's eyes and she smiled faintly, reaching out to touch the horse again. "I know just how you feel, girl. I've been there myself," she spoke quietly to the horse.

Grant laughed, but Kale's eyes narrowed suspiciously.

"I don't think I've got a three-quarter's inch wrench in that set, Pops. I'll go see if I can find one in the shed. You might need it," Kale spoke abruptly and turned to leave.

Grant stepped closer to Jacey, chuckling a bit uncertainly. "Kale's never been big on conversation." He placed a hand on Jacey's shoulder. She shrugged and smiled.

"I didn't notice," she lied, and the old man grinned. *Besides,* she added silently, *Kale really isn't the sort of man I'd care to have a conversation with.*

The mare grunted, and Jacey turned her attention back to the animal. "You're pretty miserable, aren't you, girl?"

Kale entered the barn holding another set of tools, and Grant laughed when the horse suddenly nudged Jacey. She laughed and brought her face closer to Red's.

"Well, it looks like the old girl just needed a bit of sympathy." Grant winked.

"Is this all you needed?" Kale asked gruffly.

"Sure is. Coming in for a visit tonight?" he asked his son.

"No, not tonight. I already told Mother. I've got loads of paperwork," Kale replied.

"Well, then I guess we'll see you tomorrow at church, son." Grant smiled and Kale nodded solemnly.

"Sure, I'll be there."

Grant turned toward Jacey, "And Melissa, you and Blaze are more than welcome to join us tomorrow as well. Our meeting starts at nine-thirty."

Grant smiled, and Jacey chewed on her bottom lip nervously.

What was she supposed to say? She didn't know anything about Mormons. She hadn't stepped foot in any sort of church since she was a small child, and she didn't remember it being a very agreeable experience. She could feel Kale's gaze on her, but she refused to meet his mocking glance.

"Well . . . I don't know," she began uncomfortably. "It's been a while since I've been to a church."

"Well," Grant spoke kindly, "I understand if you feel uncomfortable. Just know that it's an open invitation, and we'd love to have you come. It'd give Blaze a chance to meet a few kids his age."

Jacey felt a warm blush creep up into her cheeks, and she smiled awkwardly. "Thanks, I'll think about it," she told him, not quite able to meet his kind eyes.

"The Church was always a sore point with your dad and me. So we'll understand if you don't want to go, Melissa. There's no pressure," Grant finished. Kale glowered openly.

Jacey caught Kale's hard eyes and suddenly, determined not to let him get the best of her, she squared her shoulders and smiled at Grant. "We'll go, Uncle Grant. I know Blaze would really like to meet some other kids here."

"Wonderful!" He slapped her shoulder and turned to Kale. "Well, we'll *all* see you tomorrow, son." Grant smiled proudly as they left the barn.

Jacey caught Kale's eyes, and she smiled sweetly when he scowled. Surprised at her courage in goading Kale, she followed Grant to the Jeep and eagerly slid into the passenger seat. She closed her door and gazed out the window thoughtfully as they headed back toward Grant and Helen's home. Kale's attitude was confusing, and even more confusing was her reaction to him. Usually she wasn't so daring when it came to facing arrogant men. She felt stronger since leaving John, and she was determined not to feel inferior to another man again. Kale had a definite aversion to her, and she didn't understand it, but she wouldn't allow it to bother her. She would not be intimidated.

SEVEN

Jacey stepped in front of the long mirror that hung on the back of her bedroom door. She eyed herself critically and sighed as she adjusted her black skirt. It came just above the knee, and she suddenly wished she had a longer skirt. She pulled the waist down along her hip as low as it would go, then adjusted the seams to lay straight. She smoothed the collar of her crisp, pink blouse and brushed the length of her hair off her shoulders. She sighed. Maybe she had been too hasty in accepting Uncle Grant's invitation to church.

"Too late now," she whispered to her reflection before she clasped a heart-shaped, silver pendant around her slim neck.

It sat just below her collar bone and shone brilliantly in the morning light. She touched it gently, remembering the year Blaze had brought it home in his school bag for her. It had been her Mother's Day gift from him. He had used all his "caught-being-good bucks" from school to buy it for her. John had never observed Mother's Day, and she'd been touched when Blaze had given her the carefully wrapped gift. She treasured the pendant.

A soft knock drew Jacey's attention from her thoughts, and she called, "Come in, babe."

Blaze opened her door slowly and peeked inside.

Jacey smiled encouragingly. "You look you so nice," she told him when he entered her room.

He wore tan carpenter's pants; a black, long-sleeved shirt; and the red and gray tie he had borrowed from Kale's dresser. Blaze shrugged awkwardly, and Jacey winked playfully. "Why don't you let me fix your hair this morning?" she suggested.

She moved to her dresser to pull out a bottle of gel. She squeezed a small dab onto the palm of her hand, and Blaze stepped forward reluctantly.

"Not that stuff, Mom," he muttered, annoyed. "I'll smell like a girl."

"The smell will be gone before we even get there."

She combed through Blaze's hair with the tips of her fingers. When she finished, she wiped her hands on the bath towel she had left draped across the foot of her bed.

"There," she turned to face him, "handsome as ever."

Blaze grinned sheepishly, then muttered, "You look pretty, Mom."

A smile touched Jacey's lips. "Thank you, Blaze."

"Are you scared?" he asked, sitting on her bed.

Jacey's smile faded as she sat next to her son. She slipped her black dress shoes on her feet.

"I'm a little nervous," she admitted. She sighed and gazed out the window at the clear day. "I'm not sure what to expect."

"Because they're Mormons?" Blaze whispered.

"Well—yes. I don't know much about them," she told him honestly.

"Scott Lewis from school was a Mormon. He was nice. He didn't seem . . . weird . . . or anything," Blaze stated with a shrug.

Jacey chuckled. "I'm sure everything will be fine. Come on, we'd better go downstairs so I can help Aunt Helen with breakfast."

She stood and turned to leave before she noticed that Blaze had remained sitting. He caught her eye momentarily, then ducked his head to look down at his shoes. "What is it Blaze?" she asked, suddenly concerned.

"Nothing, I just wish—" he stopped. "I really like them, Mom," he told her.

Jacey placed her arm around his shoulders. "So do I," she said sincerely. "One day, we'll tell them the truth."

Blaze nodded and shrugged. "What if they don't like us when they know you're not Melissa?" he asked. She could hear his anxiety in the timbre of his words.

Jacey looked out the window. The day was beautiful, and it hurt to think they would have to leave here soon. Their future felt so vague, and she had truly enjoyed getting to know Grant and Helen yesterday. She sighed, turning to face Blaze. He was watching her expectantly, and she smiled a little sadly.

"I think—" she began thoughtfully, "I think maybe they will understand, Blaze. Once we tell them why we had to do it, but—" she stopped and shook her head forlornly, "we just can't tell them yet."

"Can Dad find us here?" Blaze inquired, not meeting her eyes.

She shook her head. "No, he can't. But just in case, I need to stay Melissa for a little while longer."

He nodded sadly. "I love Ocotillo, Mom. When we leave, I won't get to see him again."

Jacey sighed at the disappointment in her son's eyes. "Maybe we could visit. I don't think Uncle Grant and Aunt Helen will stay mad. They might be hurt because they think I'm Melissa, and I've lied to them, but one day I'm sure they'll understand." She hoped she was right.

"Are we going to tell them, Mom?"

"One day."

She gave him a small smile before she pulled him into another tight hug. His skinny arms wrapped about her slender waist, and Jacey tenderly kissed the top of his head.

"Are we ready for this?" she asked when he pulled away.

He shrugged. "I guess so."

• • •

Jacey gripped the steering wheel. Her hands trembled. She followed Grant and Helen's newer sedan as Grant negotiated his way through the crowded parking area. She took a deep breath when she pulled her car into a slot and shifted her Jetta into park. Jacey was surprised to see how full the parking lot was. She'd known there were a lot of Mormons in Utah, but she hadn't expected to see so many families at church.

She turned to glance at Blaze and forced a quick smile before she stepped from the car. Blaze walked at Jacey's side as they entered the large brick building with Helen and Grant. There were several people standing just inside the door and a number of children weaved in and out of their parents' legs.

Jacey smiled timidly when a few people turned their way to greet Helen and Grant. They entered a large room through tall double doors. Grant referred to it as the chapel. As they moved into the room, several people glanced at them curiously. The benches were filled with families and people of every age. Jacey looked on in amazement at the conglomeration of people as they slid into their seats. Grant had ushered Jacey into the pew first, then Blaze and himself, followed by Helen. The soft murmur of voices blended with the smooth, musical notes of an organ as people continued to enter the chapel.

Soon the music ended and a stocky, balding man stepped to the pulpit. "Good morning, brothers and sisters." He spoke, and a hush slowly fell across the chapel.

"That's Bishop Warren," Grant whispered before turning his attention back to the man speaking.

Jacey glanced around curiously. Her eyes traveled slowly across the large room. She frowned faintly when she suddenly caught sight of Kale coming through the chapel's double door. He was clean shaven and dressed in a sleek, black suit. His dark hair was gelled and styled, and Jacey couldn't help but think how different he looked today. There was no trace of the dust-covered farmer she had met yesterday.

Grant caught sight of his son. Kale paused, then nodded to Grant, just as Helen glanced his way. Her face broke into a wide grin, and she eagerly pointed to the empty spot next to Jacey. Jacey noticed Kale stiffen before he moved slowly across the back of the room and came to sit next to her.

Blaze leaned across Jacey and whispered, "Hi, Kale."

"Hey, kid." Kale glanced toward Blaze before he nodded curtly to Jacey.

The organ picked up, and a song began. Jacey grasped a green hymnal and did her best to follow along with the unfamiliar song. She nudged Blaze slightly, hoping he would join in, but he slumped in his seat. The song was titled "Precious Savior, Dear Redeemer," and its reverent words touched Jacey's heart. She felt Kale shift again, and she was surprised when his deep baritone voice joined in.

Once the song concluded, a quick prayer was offered by a young boy and a group of boys a little older than Blaze carried trays filled with bread through the congregation. Jacey looked on interestedly before Grant leaned across Blaze and quickly explained that it was the sacrament for members of their church. Jacey nodded silently and watched, fascinated, as the little metal trays were passed along each row. When a gangly, blond boy passed the tray to Kale, Jacey hesitated slightly, then relaxed as Kale passed it across her and Blaze and handed it directly to Grant. Grant caught her eye and smiled as he took the sacrament bread and passed it on to Helen.

After the sacrament was over, the bishop introduced an elderly gentleman named Brother Snips as the first speaker, and Jacey watched as the bent, old man hobbled toward the pulpit. The bishop placed a hand on the old man's shoulders and the platform lowered considerably. Brothers Snips adjusted his crooked glasses and nodded to the bishop. Bishop Warren smiled before taking his seat once again.

"Good morning," the man began in a broken, aged voice.

Jacey relaxed against her seat and listened as the man began his talk on prayer. Prayer was something that Jacey understood. She believed in Jesus Christ, although she had never attended a church. And in the past, she had often found herself praying when John's batterings and verbal attacks became too much to handle.

She was impressed with the older gentleman's talk, and she echoed the "Amen" when he concluded. She felt Kale's eyes on her, but she refused to acknowledge him. Blaze fiddled with the buttons on his shirt and slumped down in his seat when the bishop announced the rest of the meeting.

A young woman spoke on love and charity, and she was

followed by her husband who gave a powerful talk on facing the future with hope. His speech seemed as if it was meant especially for Jacey, and she hung on his every word.

He mentioned a man named Joseph Smith several times throughout his talk, recounting a few stories from the man's life. She vaguely remembered hearing about Joseph Smith. The name sounded familiar, and she was certain she had heard of him before. She wondered silently who he was and made a quick mental note to ask Grant later on. The speaker also reminded the congregation that "the perils you face will give you experience and be for your own good."

Jacey had never thought about her trials in such a way, and she was impressed at the young man's words. She was beginning to realize that she had heard nothing strange or peculiar in this meeting to validate the few rumors she'd heard in the past about Mormons. She quickly let her gaze wander around the room, then unconsciously glanced over toward Kale. She was surprised when her eyes met his, and she swiftly turned away, disturbed that he had been watching her again.

She forced her attention back toward the pulpit as the bishop announced the closing hymn. The organ's music once again filled the room, and she concentrated on singing along. An elderly woman offered the closing prayer, and Jacey smiled to herself. They had prayed four times during the one-hour meeting. She wasn't used to praying so much.

When the prayer ended, Jacey echoed the "Amen," and Blaze sat up in his seat. She smiled reassuringly just as Helen leaned over.

"Blaze, why don't you wait here with me until Sister Bates gets back?" Helen smiled, then addressed Jacey, "Sister Bates is our Primary president. She had to take her daughter out, but she'll be right back."

"Oh," Jacey replied, confused.

"Kale," Helen called, and Jacey felt him shift around to look at his mother. "Take Melissa with you to Gospel Essentials," she directed before she turned back to Jacey. "Kale teaches our Gospel Essentials class. I'll be along shortly, but I've got to find Sister Jukes. She made the most delicious rhubarb pudding last week, and I just have to have the recipe."

Jacey hesitated. She did not want to leave Grant and Helen to go alone with Kale.

Grant smiled and added, "I wish I could be in there for your first Sunday, but I teach a class of my own." He winked at Jacey and turned to give Helen's cheek an affectionate pinch before heading out the wide double doors.

Jacey looked to Blaze, and she smiled uncertainly. "Do you need me to stay with you?" she asked, trying to keep the hopeful note from her voice.

He glanced at Helen and shook his head. "No."

"Are you sure, babe?" she asked again.

"Uh-huh."

"He'll be just fine," Helen interjected quickly. "There are plenty of kids his age in Primary."

"Oh—well, okay, but if you need me I'll be—" She looked at Helen questioningly.

"She'll be in room fourteen," Helen put in promptly.

Kale stood and Jacey followed reluctantly. He waited as she slid from the pew to stand next to him. He seemed taller than ever, and Jacey felt uncomfortably dwarfed. She was easily five-seven, but he stood at least six inches taller. Kale turned immediately and led the way out of the chapel. Jacey struggled to keep up as he entered the narrow, crowded halls. He glanced back toward Jacey, then slowed to allow her to catch up to him. Several people passed and smiled as she moved to join him. He grimaced and turned to push his way through the crowd. He reached the room labeled fourteen and opened the door.

Kale grasped her elbow, and Jacey jumped when his warm, calloused hand came in contact with her skin. He pulled her into the small classroom and then turned to face her with a scowl. He looked as though he was about to speak, and Jacey eyed him skeptically. His eyes left hers to scan the room. Then he groaned and abruptly let her go before continuing up to the front of the room, leaving her standing awkwardly by a row of plastic chairs. *What was that about?* Jacey questioned as she sat. She watched mutely as Kale laid out books and pictures, preparing to teach the class.

There were only about six or seven people present, and she glanced around her uncomfortably just as a young couple sat down in the chairs next to her. She forced a quick greeting, and the woman returned her smile eagerly.

"You must be Melissa," the young woman whispered. "I'm Marcie Grace, and this is my husband, Mark."

"Oh," Jacey stammered quietly, "Hi. Yes, I am Melissa."

"How long will you be staying with Grant and Helen then?" Marcie asked curiously.

"A couple of weeks," Jacey whispered in return.

"Well, I'm so excited you're here. We live east of the Jackman place, just off the main road."

Jacey nodded. "I've noticed your place."

Marcie smiled. "It'll be fantastic having you so close. Our son Jason is about the same age as Blaze. We met Blaze when we dropped Jason off at Primary."

"That's great. I know Blaze will be excited to have someone to play with while we're here," Jacey responded.

"Jason will. He was so excited when Grant told us you and your son were coming. There aren't too many kids his age to play with, since we don't live in town and all, you know."

"Brother Grace, would you care to offer the opening prayer?" Kale suddenly spoke. Jacey smiled at Marcie Grace before she turned her attention toward the front of the room.

A sudden hush fell across the classroom, and Mark stood to offer a quick prayer. A few moments later, Helen bustled into the room and sat down next to Jacey. Jacey smiled, relieved to see Helen's familiar face. Helen patted Jacey's knee and leaned over to greet Marcie.

Kale began his lesson, and Jacey was amazed at how quickly the hour-long class slipped by. Kale seemed like a different man during the lesson. He smiled openly at the people in the classroom. Many commented or offered insights, and everyone in the room seemed to really like and respect him. Jacey suddenly grimaced at the thought. John had been able to turn his charm on and off like a switch too. Nobody, not even his family, had suspected what was going on behind her and John's closed door. She shook her head, forcing her thoughts back to Kale's lesson on faith. She had never thought about her faith before, and it was an interesting thing to consider. She wanted to hear more on the subject when the lesson was over.

"Oh, Melissa," Marcie said once the closing prayer had concluded. "Why don't you and Blaze come over for lunch tomorrow? Mark said Kale will be coming by to help him fix his work truck. You and Blaze could ride down with him and spend a few hours while they get that hunk of junk working."

"Oh," Jacey stammered, unsure what to say.

"That would be wonderful," Helen stepped in quickly. "It would give Blaze and Jason time to play together and give you a chance for some young company." She patted Jacey's arm and stepped around Marcie.

Now what am I supposed to say? Jacey wondered quickly. Marcie turned an expectant smile her way. Jacey forced a grin and nodded. "That would be great. We'd enjoy that."

"Fantastic! We'll see you tomorrow then," Marcie said. "I'd better get now and check on my little rascals." She waved as she left the room.

EIGHT

John Trent sat idly, staring out the large window of the Hyatt's presidential suite. The day was clear and blue, and the downtown Detroit traffic was thick. He liked this city. He raised his hand to take another long drag on his fat Arturo Don Carlos cigar. He relished the sweet taste before he exhaled a large cloud of smoke, filling the room with the cigar's toasty aroma. He had always enjoyed a good cigar, and Don Carlos was the best. The Hyatt also seemed to offer the best—the best of Detroit—and that was exactly what he deserved: the best. He had worked hard to get where he was, and nothing was going to stand in his way, especially not Jacey.

It was time to get his boy back. He had given that woman everything. A luxurious home, nice cars, elegant clothes, and she had betrayed him. She had taken his son. Did she really believe she was smart enough to hide Blaze from him? She had always been stupid. She had constantly made mistakes, and he'd always been more than lenient with her, but now he would really make her pay.

He stood and took another drag on the cigar as he stalked toward the large window. Jacey was out there, somewhere, and he couldn't wait to get his hands on her one last time. He laughed quietly to himself just as a loud knock sounded on the suite's door. Taking one last drag, he stubbed the cigar out, placing it in the ashtray. He reached the door, and his hand automatically moved to the inside pocket of his luxurious suit coat. His fingers rested against the cool metal of his .25 caliber.

"Who is it?"

"It's me," a gravelly voice called.

John opened the door, and Rafael Vizcaino entered the large suite. He nodded mutely to John before he walked toward the wet bar to pour himself a bourbon. John stared at Rafael in silence for a short moment. He watched as Rafael stirred the ice into his drink. A slight smile played at the corner of the older man's mouth.

"Well?" John asked abruptly.

Rafael downed his drink. "Well, what?" he asked with a grimace. He walked across the Oriental rug to a black armchair by the window and sat down, squeezing his bulk into it.

"Did you find Salvatore?" John pressed, irritated.

"Yeah, I found him, but we'll meet later, down in Archimedes. Told him we'd have drinks, talk." Rafael eyed John carefully.

"I told you before. Salvatore's no beefer. I've worked with him before. He's good people, Ralph."

Rafael shrugged his thick shoulders. "We'll talk tomorrow." He rubbed a finger across his well-trimmed goatee and smiled at John. "Relax."

John scowled before he turned toward the bar for a drink.

"Fine," John muttered. He dropped ice into his glass and splashed the thick, amber liquid across the cubes.

"You just can't wait, can you?" Rafael chuckled.

John shook his head before he took a drink. The whiskey burned the back of his throat. "I want my boy back." He cleared his throat and poured himself another half a glass.

"You had better hope that boy of yours hasn't beefed." Rafael stood to retrieve a cigar from the humidor on the ornate side table.

"My boy ain't no squealer. Besides, he didn't see nothing. I left him in the car."

"All the same, I hope for your sake he hasn't talked." Rafael lit his cigar, then took a long drag. Smoke curled out from his nose and mouth. "I don't want the boss on our backs over your mistake."

• • •

Jacey woke with a start. She sat up quickly, her heart racing as she strained her ears against the quiet. She heard Blaze moan and bolted from her bed into his room. He was dreaming again. She approached the edge of his bed and laid her hand against his cheek. He cried out, and Jacey shook him, calling his name tenderly.

"Blaze, honey, wake up." She shook him again.

"No!" he called out before his eyes shot open. Fear clouded his expression, and Jacey gathered him to her.

"Blaze, baby, you were dreaming," she whispered as she pressed his trembling body against her.

"Mom." She heard Blaze's muffled sob. His arms shot around her, and he clung to her.

"Shhh, honey, it's all right. You were only dreaming. It was only a dream." She pressed a kiss against the top of his head.

Silent sobs shook his body, and she held him tighter. He hadn't had a nightmare in weeks. She'd hoped his bad dreams would stop once she left John, but they hadn't.

She held him for a while longer before she asked quietly, "Can you tell me about it, Blaze?"

He hiccupped and shook his head.

Jacey sighed. "Sweetheart," she encouraged, "it would help to talk about it. Can you tell Momma about it?"

Blaze mutely shook his head again. His thin arms still held her tightly. She pressed a kiss against his damp forehead and faintly rocked back and forth. She held him for several long minutes before she realized he had fallen back asleep. His head rested against her chest. His hair stood in untidy tufts, and his brow was beaded in perspiration. She kissed his head again, then shifted her body so she could stand. As she tucked Blaze back into bed, he sighed in his sleep, and she gently laid his head against his pillow.

Jacey watched his face, relaxed in sleep, for a moment. Then she rubbed her hand gently across his soft cheek. She felt so helpless, and she couldn't seem to shake the uneasy feeling that Blaze was hiding something from her. She couldn't get him to open up about his feelings, even though she desperately wanted to talk to him about his father. Jacey knew the divorce hadn't been easy on him, but things had seemed to take a turn for the worse several months before then. What had happened? What was he feeling? She leaned down to place one last feather-light kiss against his clammy forehead. Tears filled her eyes as she gazed down at her sleeping child. She brushed at a stray tear, then stood and returned to her room.

Back in her own room, she moved to peer out the window at the darkened sky. A sliver of a moon was out, and the sky was thick with stars. She could hear the low whistle of a train in the distance. The sound seemed so lonely. She sighed and stared up at the milky waves that streaked across the inky blackness. She had never seen so many stars. The never-ending brightness of the city always hid them from view. It was an amazing sight. She let her eyes stray out across the pastures. One single light shone brightly against the hillside, and Jacey fleetingly wondered what Kale was doing awake at such a late hour. She groaned quietly, then shut the curtains and crawled back into the bed, pulling the thick covers across her. Gradually she fell into a restless sleep.

• • •

In the morning, Jacey woke with a headache. She felt unsteady and sore, and she realized that she had overslept. She moaned and rolled over, covering her head with her quilt to shield her eyes from the bright light spilling into the room. From somewhere in the distance, she could hear the muffled sound of Blaze's laughter and Grant's deep, rumbling voice.

She lay there for a few more minutes before resolutely throwing back the covers. Her bed-side clock read nine-thirty. Groggily, she pulled herself out of bed and stumbled to the bathroom for a quick shower. The hot water helped to ease her aching head and wash away the hazy remnants of too much sleep. Once back in her room, she dressed quickly before she searched her purse to find her painkillers. She shook two from the bottle and slipped them into her pocket to take after breakfast. Then she dried her hair and left it hanging loose. Its length spilled down across her back in soft waves, and she took another moment to apply a touch of makeup. She gave herself a cursory glance in the mirror before she turned toward the window.

Jacey could still hear Blaze and Grant, and she wondered curiously what they were up to. She peered down at the yard, squinting against the bright sunlight. Blaze was over by the corrals talking to Grant. Grant threw back his head and laughed at something Blaze said, and Jacey smiled. It still surprised her that Blaze had taken to Grant so quickly.

She hoped that with a good male role model, Blaze might open up about his feelings concerning John. She knew that Blaze loved John. John had always been a caring father. She and John had been very happy after Blaze was born, and John had spoiled him terribly. Most days after work, John had tickled and played with Blaze, and as Blaze had grown older, John had begun to take him to work quite often. Blaze loved going to the restaurants with John, and they had been close. But the older Blaze got, the more upset he had become about John's treatment of Jacey. Jacey knew Blaze hated it when John lost his temper, and she'd usually find him hiding in his closet or under his bed after she and John had had a bad fight.

Jacey hated that Blaze had seen John hit her, and she often sensed that Blaze carried a terrible burden on his young shoulders, but their life with John hadn't always been terrible. At times, John would go for months without hitting her, and during those times, he always seemed like the man she had first married. He had pampered and spoiled her with new clothes and jewelry, and she and Blaze had loved John's sense of humor.

There had been times when John had held her and loved her. In those moments, she had truly felt as if they were a family. He had taken them to the movies and plays. They had even gone to Disney World more than once together. When John's temper became unbearable, she had clung to those memories. She had loved the man he could be, but more and more often, toward the end, he had become the man she was so terribly frightened of. That last beating, she had truly believed he was going to kill her.

Blaze must have thought so too. He had never run for help before. Was that why he was so frightened of John now? No, she shook her head. Blaze had withdrawn even before that last fight. But why? She sat down on her bed and stared unseeing out the window. She raised a hand to her aching head and sighed.

What can I do? It would be hard for any child to lose a parent, and she had cut Blaze off from John completely. Was that wrong? Blaze's nightmares, she thought, had begun to ease after the first few months at Melissa's, but last night . . . . Had running away been a terrible thing to do?

No. She'd had to cut Blaze off from John, and now, with what the FBI had told her, she had to keep Blaze away from him. But she really had no proof that what the FBI had told her was true. Then again, she had never liked Rafael, not at all. She just didn't know what to think.

Blaze's attitude had been getting progressively worse in Detroit, but just the few days they had spent in Helen and Grant's house had seemed to truly make a difference. He was smiling and laughing again, and he seemed to really love the Jackmans.

Jacey covered her face with trembling hands and rubbed her aching temples. She needed to go eat breakfast so she could take the aspirin and get rid of her annoying headache. She stood, determined to shake her disturbing thoughts, and made her way downstairs. An unusually quiet and empty kitchen met her, and Jacey glanced around, confused before she saw the bright yellow note sitting in the middle of the table. Jacey reached over and read it.

Melissa,
 Gone into town for a few groceries—won't be gone long. I left you some breakfast; it's keeping warm in the oven. Blaze helped me make your pancake.
Love,
Aunt Helen.
PS—fresh O.J. hiding behind the milk in the fridge.

Jacey smiled to herself. She moved to the stove and pulled out an oversized, warm plate. She laughed out loud when she saw her smiley-face pancake. Two small eggs had been used for the eyes, a thick strip of bacon formed a crooked smile, and a crisp hash brown patty, cut in half, worked as the ears. She couldn't help but smile. She felt better already. She located the pitcher of orange juice that Helen had mentioned and poured herself a generous glass before sitting at the table to enjoy her breakfast.

She finished her pancake and was just about to start on her hash browns when the washroom door suddenly banged open. Jacey jumped, startled at the unexpected noise. She glanced over, expecting to see Blaze, but her eyes widened slightly when Kale paused in the doorway. He looked caught off guard. Then his eyes narrowed, and he frowned. Jacey hesitated before she squared her shoulders and spoke.

"Good morning, Kale."

He faltered slightly before nodding at her.

"Morning," he muttered as he stepped into the kitchen.

He moved to the sink and squatted down to examine the pipes underneath. Without another glance her way, he stood and walked back outside. Jacey shook her head, bewildered, and returned to her breakfast. A few moments later, Kale entered the kitchen again. This time he held a shiny metal toolbox in one hand and a heavy wrench in the other.

He sat his tools down on the hardwood floor with a loud chink before he scooted under the sink on his back. His long legs stuck out, and his thick shoulders filled the tiny cabinet. It looked uncomfortable. Jacey watched him for a moment before she picked her plate of half-eaten breakfast off the table. She didn't dare try to make her way toward the sink, so she placed her plate of food on the counter and turned to go back upstairs.

"Don't mind me. Sit back down and finish your breakfast."

Kale's deep voice startled Jacey, and she paused. She turned and grasped her plate again, then moved automatically, to sit down at the table. She sat down before she realized she was following orders. John had always dictated what she should or shouldn't do, and she had always been quick to obey him. She stood suddenly, determined not to allow another man to control her actions again.

"I'll finish outside, thank you," she told him crisply as she moved toward the door. She stepped awkwardly around his long legs and gave him a quick side glance. Kale was watching her.

His scowl deepened before he replied. "Fine by me. I just didn't want you to feel like I was chasing you out of the kitchen, that's all."

Jacey paused. She could feel a sudden blush touch her cheeks and she said quickly, "Oh, well, thank you."

She turned away and rushed outside, letting the screen door bang shut before she moved toward the picnic table to sit under the shade of the large cottonwood. As she sat down she exhaled noisily and glanced at her half-eaten breakfast. *What a morning.* She pushed her plate away and leaned her forearms against the smooth, aged wood. A warm breeze played through her hair, and she could hear the soft drone of a bee buzzing close by.

She sighed as she laid her head down against her arms. That man had a way of upsetting her. He didn't like her, that much was obvious, but why did it bother her so badly? Was it Melissa he didn't like or was it herself? She groaned, feeling dejected. Why did she react to him so strongly? He wasn't really like John, but he seemed to get her dander up every time he came around.

Jacey was not looking forward to this afternoon. She didn't want to ride over with Kale to Marcie Grace's house. She wondered if she and Blaze should just drive there themselves.

"Hi, Mom."

Blaze's voice caused Jacey to raise her head. He bounded across the yard toward her, and she sat up and plastered a smile on her face.

"Hey, babe," she greeted him.

He grinned as he sat down across from her. "Guess what?"

Jacey was pleased to see that all traces of last night were gone from his face, and she couldn't help but laugh at his obvious enthusiasm.

"What?" she asked.

"I gathered all the eggs this morning, and I fed Ocotillo from my hands again," he told her. He pointed to her plate. "Are you going to eat that?" he asked hopefully.

"No, I'm finished, but it was the best breakfast I've ever eaten. My little pancake man looked so good. I hated to eat him."

She smiled when Blaze eagerly popped the rest of her bacon into his mouth.

"Good," he said with his mouth full. "I'm starving."

"That's because a boys' legs are hollow. I bet you didn't know that." Grant laughed as he approached them.

Jacey glanced up, startled. She smiled a quick greeting. "Good morning, Uncle Grant."

He came around to give her an affectionate squeeze on her shoulders. His rough, warm hands felt comforting to Jacey, and she looked up into his craggy, grinning face.

"Morning, sunshine." He laughed just as the back door swung open and Kale stepped out into the yard with his tools.

Grant turned and greeted Kale. "Morning, son."

Kale nodded to Grant as he approached the table.

"Hi, Kale," Blaze said enthusiastically.

"Morning, Pops. Hey, kid." Kale grinned at Blaze, then playfully tipped the brim of Blaze's wide cowboy hat.

Blaze laughed, but Jacey inhaled sharply, disturbed by the playful exchange between Kale and her son.

Kale turned back to Grant and explained, "It's going again. Tell Mom if it gives her anymore trouble, we should probably just replace it. The flange and the gasket are fairly corroded, but the drain line's fixed."

"Hmm." Grant rubbed his stubble-covered chin. "Well, what do you think? Should we just go ahead and replace it now?"

Kale nodded. "I would. I'm not sure how much more that old disposal can take."

"I'll take Mother into Provo next week and let her pick out a new one," Grant said thoughtfully.

"Let me know when you've got it. I'll come put it in when I get back from Alaska," Kale replied before he turned toward Jacey. "Mark said you wanted a lift out to their place today?"

"Oh—well, yes. Marcie asked if Blaze and I could come for lunch since you'll be driving out to help her husband, but if it's a problem, we can just take our own car," she responded.

"It's no problem," he replied abruptly. "I'll be leaving around noon. I'll stop by to get you then."

Kale turned his attention back to Grant. "I'd better get on back so I can check Red. Her foal should come tonight; at least

I'm hoping it comes tonight. I'd hate leaving tomorrow if she doesn't drop today."

Grant nodded. "Well, if she doesn't, I'll stay out at your place until she does."

"Thanks, Dad."

"So how long is this run going to be?" Grant asked.

Kale shrugged. "Hopefully only a week, but Barton and Allen want to open a couple of old fields. I need to complete full surveys on the areas, check the stability and effect of reopening. I'll be staying in Wasilla if you need to reach me."

Jacey silently listened to the exchange. *What sort of work does Kale do?* Jacey thought.

Grant nodded thoughtfully. "I'll swing by tonight to see how things are going with the mare."

"Thanks," Kale said before he turned again to Jacey. "I'll be back in an hour or so, Melissa."

Jacey winced inside at being called Melissa. "Thanks," she said.

Blaze bounced with excitement. "Jason says their cat just had kittens. I've never held a real baby kitty before. And they've got four-wheelers too, Mom. Jason says he'll take me for a ride. They're so cool. Maybe Jason will let me drive," he finished breathlessly.

Jacey stared at her son with wide eyes. "What's a four-wheeler?" she asked.

"An ATV—All-Terrain Vehicle," Grant explained.

"Ah." Jacey nodded. "Well, we'll see Blaze. I'm not sure I like the idea of you being on one of those without a grown-up."

"Oh!" Blaze whined, and Kale's mouth quirked slightly. "Come on, Mom!"

" 'We will see,' I said," she replied with a small laugh. "We're not even there yet. Now, why don't you go on in and take a shower so we can be ready when Kale comes back."

Blaze frowned. "I don't need a shower. I had one yesterday. Besides, we cowboys are supposed to be dirty."

Jacey shook her head, exasperated, and Grant laughed loudly.

She heard Kale's laughter join Grant's before he spoke up. "That's right, kid." Kale grinned and patted his own dusty jeans.

He continued to chuckle as he turned toward the sheds and walked away.

Blaze eyed Jacey's exasperated expression mischievously, and Jacey couldn't hide her grin before she pointed toward the house. "Shower."

Blaze's face fell. "Oh, all right." He stood to move sluggishly toward the house.

Jacey watched, amused, as her son opened the backdoor and disappeared inside. Grant laughed again and sat down across from Jacey. The table shifted under his weight, and Jacey turned to smile at the older man.

"Kid's got a point." Grant winked, and Jacey shook her head in mock frustration.

"He's really enjoying this," Jacey said, then paused. "I hope he isn't keeping you from other work." She pulled her breakfast plate back toward her, pinched off a piece of cold hash brown, and popped it in her mouth.

"'Course not," Grant responded cheerfully. "Besides, Kale does most of the real tough stuff when he's around. When he's gone, Mark Grace comes over. My old bones just aren't up to too much these days."

Jacey nodded thoughtfully. She was curious about Kale and his work, but she hesitated to ask. Then, resolutely, she went on, "Kale's going to Alaska?"

"He sure is. He spends a quite a bit of time up there, working with the big oil companies. He's usually gone no more than a week or two at a time. He does inspections on the land and such, but he completes most of his paperwork here at home. That way he can be back to work the farm and his stock."

Jacey paused before she asked, "He's a geologist, right? I remember you mentioning he was."

"He is, and a darn good one too. He loves the land—has since he was just a kid. Mother could hardly keep that boy inside." Grant chuckled softly, and his eyes shone with memories.

"Alaska would be very exciting."

"He loves it. And the work has been good for him, especially since Adrian's death. It's helped him to stay busy."

Jacey's eyes narrowed, confused. "Adrian?"

"Kale's wife—she died four years ago in an accident. You didn't know?"

Jacey's heart pounded suddenly. Melissa hadn't told her about Kale or his sister, Allison, let alone Kale's wife. She opened her mouth to reply, then shut it and shook her head mutely.

"Aw, well—" Grant shrugged. "—it was a while ago. Kale took it pretty hard though. We all did."

"I'm so sorry," Jacey replied quietly.

"It was tough on all of us. But Kale seems to be doing better. He's back to church, and he's gone out on a few dates with a local girl named Cindy. He doesn't say much, but I think things could be getting a little more serious between the two of them." He paused, then added thoughtfully, "And I hope it is. It would be good to see Kale married again. Every man needs a good woman to lean on. Without you women, we're pretty lost."

Jacey was surprised to discover Kale had been married before. Was that why he seemed so withdrawn? Grief affected everyone differently. She silently wondered about his new girlfriend, Cindy. What sort of woman was she?

"What about you, Melissa?" Grant suddenly asked, and Jacey looked up, startled. "Any serious relationships since Spencer and you broke apart?"

"Oh—well," Jacey stammered, caught off guard, "No—no, not really." She could feel a warm blush begin to creep into her cheeks.

Grant nodded and cleared his throat gruffly. "Well, it's probably none of my business, but does that man ever come around? I mean—I haven't heard the boy mention his old man once."

The rhythm of her heart suddenly picked up again, and she swallowed hard before replying carefully, "No, he doesn't come around often. He and Blaze aren't very close anymore."

"Ah, well, that's too bad."

"Yes, it is," Jacey muttered self-consciously.

NINE

Nick Salvatore approached from across the Hyatt's expansive lobby, and Rafael stood, watching the man closely. Salvatore shook John's hand before he turned to Rafael with a mocking smile.

"Rafael," he acknowledged.

"Sal," Rafael responded coldly, eyeing the younger man with evident distaste.

"Good to see you, Sal. How's Cross?" John asked quietly.

Salvatore shrugged. "He's away."

John nodded thoughtfully. "Too bad."

Salvatore shrugged knowingly, and John gestured toward Archimedes, the Hyatt's exclusive bar.

"Let's talk." John grinned, and the men turned toward the bar.

They found a table in the back of the large room. The tavern was fairly empty, and that pleased John. The quicker he could get Sal's cooperation, the sooner he could get his hands on Jacey.

A waitress approached the three men and took their drink orders. While they waited for their drinks to arrive, John and Sal caught up on their common acquaintances, and Rafael sat silently, enjoying the rest of his cigar.

"So, Vizcaino says you've got a job needs done?" Sal spoke quietly once the waitress had delivered their drinks and left.

John nodded, reaching into his suit pocket to remove a folded envelope. He gave it one final glance before he slid it across the table to Nick Salvatore.

"You're good people, Sal. I can expect it soon?" John asked. Sal grinned knowingly and slipped the envelope inside his pocket. John leaned forward, and he eyed the surrounding tables. "Find her," he snarled dangerously.

Sal laughed malevolently before saying, "I'll get the street crew working."

He grinned and raised his drink toward John. The tawny liquid sparkled in Sal's glass. John sat back in his seat with a satisfied smirk.

• • •

"Is Kale here yet?" Blaze called as he bounded down the stairs and into the kitchen. Jacey and Helen were busy putting the groceries away.

Jacey shook her head. "No, not yet." A sudden rush of nerves tickled her stomach.

"I can't wait to see Jason's kitties," Blaze said. Then he added quickly, "Mom, these shoes are getting too tight."

Jacey glanced his way, "We'll have to get you some new ones. Maybe we'll drive into town tomorrow."

"Can I get a pair of real cowboy boots like Kale's and Uncle Grant's?" Blaze asked, his tone hopeful.

Kale suddenly walked into the kitchen, and Jacey turned to him with startled eyes before turning back toward Blaze. "I don't know. We'll have to see if we can find any."

"Find what?" Kale asked nonchalantly as he pulled a grape from one of Helen's sacks. He popped it in his mouth, then turned to Helen and hugged her tightly.

"Cowboy boots," Jacey answered.

"Yeah," Blaze jumped in. "I wanna get some just like yours."

Kale laughed openly, and Jacey stared for a moment. She hadn't heard him laugh so freely. She ducked her head to hide her surprise and swiftly focused her attention back on the groceries. She liked the way Kale's laugh sounded.

"You want some boots, do you? Well, I bet I could help you

find some." He turned to Jacey, "There's a Western wear store in Spanish Fork. It's not too far from here. They carry kids' sizes."

"Oh," Jacey said, nodding, "all right. Thank you, Kale."

"Yes, that's right. It isn't too far from here. I bet Grant knows the exit. It's a little store just on Main Street," Helen suddenly remembered.

"That would be great," Jacey agreed quietly.

Blaze stood and moved into the kitchen just as Kale asked, "You ready to go, kid?"

Blaze nodded enthusiastically, and he and Jacey followed Kale out into the thick afternoon heat. She was surprised to discover a newer, large Dodge truck parked next to Helen and Grant's modest sedan. Its bright red paint gleamed in the sun. Kale walked to the passenger side, and Blaze gawked openly at the truck.

"Wow," Blaze breathed. "Cool truck."

"You think so, huh?" Kale replied dryly. The corners of his mouth twitched slightly.

"Can I drive?" Blaze asked, grinning.

"Blaze," Jacey admonished quietly.

"I was just kidding! Jeez, Mom." Blaze scowled and Kale chuckled.

Kale opened the passenger side door and ushered Blaze in before he turned to offer his hand to Jacey. Startled, Jacey paused, then grasped his offered hand, allowing him to help her into the high truck.

"Thank you," she said, feeling oddly breathless.

She could smell the musky scent of his aftershave, and his hand felt warm against hers. He seemed so tall. He was much taller than John. Kale nodded curtly and he hastily shut the door. He jumped in the large truck with ease and settled his long legs into the driver's seat comfortably.

Grant suddenly appeared from around the sheds, and Kale rolled down his window to call out to him. "I'll arrange every-thing with Mark for the rest of this week."

Grant waved and Kale turned the key. The truck growled to life, and Jacey felt the engine's powerful rumble. She gazed around at the expensive interior. A top-of-the-line CD player adorned the wide dash, and a navigation system held Blaze's attention.

"Cool. What's this?" Blaze asked.

Kale shifted in his seat to back the truck out of the driveway. He expertly swung the large truck around to face the long dirt road, and then answered, "GPS—it's a navigation system. Tells you where you are and where you need to go. Watch." He flipped a button and the screen came to life. "See that? That's us. This line is the road that we're on right now. This area is Nephi. It's a town just south of us. Jason's house is right here, where the lines intersect," Kale explained patiently.

"Wow, cool," Blaze replied excitedly. "Dad never had—" Blaze suddenly stopped, and Jacey paled visibly. Blaze's eyes widened with fear, and he turned quickly to Jacey. Jacey inhaled and smiled awkwardly.

Kale's eyes suddenly shot to Jacey's face, and he watched her for a short moment before he asked Blaze, "Your dad never had what?"

"A GPS," Blaze muttered. He ducked his head, and Kale's eyes narrowed.

Jacey laughed nervously, then smiled openly at Blaze. "Your dad had one. He just never used it. That's why we got lost all the time."

Blaze raised his eyes toward hers and smiled briefly, but Jacey caught Kale's questioning gaze. His eyes shot toward Blaze and then back to Jacey as his mouth twisted wryly.

"Yeah," Blaze added, and Jacey slipped her arm around his shoulder.

It was the first reference he had made to his father in a long time, but Jacey hoped it wouldn't happen again around Kale or the Jackmans. It could easily give them away.

They finished the drive in awkward silence, and Jacey breathed a sigh of relief when Kale pulled his Dodge into Marcie's wide driveway.

"Here we are," Kale said, jumping from the truck.

Jacey reached for the door just as she realized Kale had come around to her side, intent on helping her down. He opened the door and extended his hand. She took it and allowed him to help her out. He did the same for Blaze, and Jacey wondered at the gesture. She had never had a man open her car door. It was something she had always wanted John to do, but he never had.

Jacey stepped around the large truck and studied the Graces' house. It was a sage green manufactured home and fairly new. Flowerbeds framed the house, and several wooden boxes filled with brightly colored flowers adorned the windows. The door opened, and Marcie peered out.

"I thought I heard you pull in." She smiled a greeting as she came out onto the porch.

"Afternoon, Marcie. Is Mark around?" Kale inquired.

"He's out back," Marcie indicated with a wave of her hand, "tinkering with that truck."

Kale nodded, then tipped his hat. He turned to Jacey, and she smiled tentatively. He nodded brusquely before he walked away to find Mark.

"I'm so glad you came. Jason's driving me nuts. He's been asking about you all morning, Blaze," Marcie called, descending the stairs.

Blaze shuffled his feet uncomfortably but perked up when Jason suddenly appeared, standing in the doorway. "Good, you're here!" Jason bounded out the door and down the steps.

The boy was slightly taller than Blaze, and he had a bright shock of nearly white hair. He grinned as he approached Blaze. "Wanna see the kitties?" he asked.

Blaze nodded eagerly. "Yeah."

Marcie laughed. "Well, go on back and see them, but stay out of Dad's way, Jason."

Marcie and Jacey grinned at one another knowingly as the boys quickly raced around the house and out of sight.

"Why don't you come on in? I've almost got lunch ready." Marcie said and Jacey turned to follow.

Lunch was a veritable feast. Marcie had prepared a pork roast with roasted potatoes and carrots. Jacey helped put together a fresh leaf salad, and Marcie pulled a huge pan of brownies out of the oven just before she called the men and the kids in to the table. Blaze followed behind Jason, and Michael, Marcie's-five-year-old, followed Blaze to the table. Jacey was surprised when Marcie left the room and returned holding a two-year-old boy. She introduced Michael and then the baby, Christopher.

"Three boys," Marcie lamented with a grin. "I can't wait to get a girl."

Jacey laughed. "I had no idea you had three."

Mark chuckled as he joined the conversation. "They're a handful."

The conversation around the table was limited as they all enjoyed the meal Marcie had prepared. When they were finished, Kale and Mark disappeared again. Jacey and Marcie worked on cleaning up, then Marcie grabbed Christopher, and the three of them joined the other boys outside under a large oak tree. Marcie pulled two worn lawn chairs out of a nearby shed, and they sat down to watch the kids play. Jason, Michael, and Blaze were swinging on a tire attached to the old tree, and Jacey could hear Mark and Kale's muffled voices as they worked on Mark's truck further away from the house. She heard Kale laugh over something that Mark said and couldn't help but wonder what they were talking about.

"I bet you I can get this ball through the hole."

Jacey turned to watch as Jason grabbed a football lying in the grass. He threw the ball, missing the hole. Blaze laughed as he chased the ball, and Jacey smiled when Blaze threw the ball.

"Aw, man!" he yelled with a grin as he missed the tire.

Jason ran to retrieve the ball as it bounced across the yard. "Come on, try again, Blaze." He tossed the ball to Blaze, and Jacey laughed quietly. It was so good to see Blaze having a good time. She was glad that they had come.

• • •

"Thank you for the nice lunch, Marcie. I really enjoyed it." Jacey smiled at her new friend as she stepped out onto the front porch. Marcie gave her a quick hug. Surprised, Jacey returned the embrace.

"Come again soon. It's been so nice to visit with you," Marcie returned.

It was nearing five o'clock, and Jacey was grateful to be getting back. She felt tired after sitting in the heat most of the afternoon, and Blaze looked worn out from playing. They drove the few minutes back to the Jackman's farm in silence, and Jacey stared out toward the open fields. Golden fields were touched by blue sky. It was beautiful here. Life seemed to move at a slower pace. It was something Jacey wasn't used to, but she didn't mind it in the least. It was nice to look out across open pastures instead of a maze of towering sky scrapers and thick, bumper-to-bumper traffic. She smiled slightly, thinking that Melissa would have gone mad by now.

The nearest mall, according to Aunt Helen, was close to thirty miles away, and Jacey couldn't imagine that the market in Nephi would be all that appealing to someone used to big city shopping centers. Jacey fleetingly wondered what life in Salt Lake would be like. It was a much smaller city than either Chicago or Detroit, but she still wasn't looking forward to the move back to a fast-paced city life.

Jacey sighed quietly when Kale pulled his truck into the drive-way. The front door opened immediately, and Helen stepped out onto the porch. She leaned across the railing and waved.

Blaze stirred eagerly. "I've got to go feed Ocotillo."

"I left a bucket of oats by the gate before we left. Give him a bit of those," Kale said as he parked the truck and cut the engine. He opened his door and stepped out onto the gravel.

Blaze followed Kale out the driver-side door, waved quickly to Helen, and raced around the side of the house toward the corral. Jacey opened her door and was once again surprised when Kale appeared to help her down.

"Will you be staying for supper tonight, son?" Jacey heard Helen call as Kale grasped her elbow to assist her out of the truck.

Kale's hand tightened slightly against Jacey's arm. The warmth of his large hand penetrated the fabric of her blouse. His hand lingered as he turned his attention to Helen.

"No, Mom. I really need to get back to check on Red, and I've got a bit more paperwork to sort out before tomorrow," he called back.

Jacey stirred slightly, then moved to pull her elbow from his grasp. Realizing he was still holding Jacey, Kale's eyes shot toward hers. She met his gaze, questioningly. He abruptly let her go and stepped away. As he moved toward the porch, Jacey grimaced slightly. She shut the truck door and followed.

"Hi, Melissa. Did you have a good visit then?" Helen greeted as Jacey stepped up into the cool shade of the porch.

"I did, thank you," she replied.

Helen smiled and gave her a quick friendly pat on the back before she turned her attention back to Kale. Kale frowned slightly as he leaned against the porch railing and gazed out toward the mountains in the distance.

"Dad checked on Red an hour ago, son. Why don't you just stay for a quick bite?" Helen pleaded.

Kale sighed and turned to face his mother. He opened his mouth to reply just as Helen continued, cutting him off, "The potatoes only need to boil for another ten minutes or so, and besides, you need at least one good meal before you go tramping off in them backwoods. You simply don't eat right when you're out there."

A slow smile replaced Kale's dour expression. "All right, Mother. You win. I'll stay for supper." He walked toward her and placed a quick kiss on her plump cheek. "You know, you worry too much." He grinned and Helen laughed.

"I'll always be your mother. You'll never be too old for me to worry about," Helen reminded him with a teasing glare.

Jacey couldn't help but feel relieved that Kale was leaving tomorrow. She and Blaze would be gone by the time he returned.

• • •

"Melissa."

Jacey stirred slightly.

"Melissa."

The voice seemed to come from some distance away, and Jacey moaned quietly as a hand grasped her shoulder.

Her eyes flew open, and she instinctively jerked away from the man standing above her. She let out a startled gasp before her mind registered Kale's face peering down at her. His brown eyes watched her skeptically, and she sat up straight, raising a hand to her beating chest. She glanced about her quickly, trying to clear the confusion from her mind.

After returning from Marcie's, Jacey had decided to rest in the living room for a few moments. She must have fallen asleep.

"Are you all right?" Kale's asked. Taking a step back, he eyed her suspiciously.

She took a quick breath and laughed self-consciously, "I'm— I'm sorry. I didn't realize where I was for a moment. I must have been dreaming. I—well, I usually don't fall asleep like that."

Kale watched her closely for a moment before he spoke, "Look, I—" He paused and a scowl marred his face. "Dinner's ready," he finished curtly.

"Oh, okay—thank you," Jacey stammered when he turned abruptly toward the kitchen, leaving her alone in the living room.

She shook her head, confused, and raised a trembling hand to brush the hair back off her damp forehead. Then she stood and took a moment to stretch the muscles in her back and reorient her mind before she entered the dining room. Heaping bowls of steaming asparagus and mashed potatoes decorated the dinner table, and she breathed in the fragrant aroma of melting butter.

She smiled sheepishly when Helen moved toward the table carrying a platter with steaming, fresh-baked rolls.

"I just hated to have Kale wake you," Helen commented cheerfully as she placed the platter in the middle of the table, next to the asparagus.

Jacey laughed self-consciously. "I didn't realize I was so tired," she confessed, glancing at Kale. His back was to her as he washed his hands, and Jacey quickly added, "What can I do to help?"

"Everything's ready. I'm just about to pull the casserole from the oven." Helen smiled and patted Jacey's arm as she walked past.

Kale shut the water off and turned to face the dining area. He dried his hand on a dish towel before throwing it casually onto the countertop. Jacey caught his eye as she glanced around, wondering where Grant and Blaze were.

Seeming to read her thoughts, Kale suddenly informed her,

"He'll be in. He and Pops are just coming up the lane. Blaze went with him to get the tractor."

"I see. Well, in that case, I think I'll go and wash up before they get here," Jacey replied.

She turned and made her way up the stairs, then sighed as she shut the door to her room. When she caught sight of her disheveled appearance in the mirror above the dresser, she grimaced. Her hair was a tangled mess, and dark mascara was smudged under both eyes. She groaned and quickly reached for her comb.

Jacey sighed. "I think you've bit off more than you can chew," she muttered to her reflection before she sank onto the edge of the bed.

She felt anxious to get into town tomorrow. The time away from the Jackmans would give her a good opportunity to pick up a newspaper. She needed to look into jobs and apartments in Salt Lake City.

"Mom," Jacey heard Blaze's familiar voice call out from the dining room below.

"Coming," she answered before she gave herself another cursory glance in the mirror.

Satisfied with her quick fix, she bounded down the stairs to join Blaze and the others. She caught sight of Blaze's grinning face when she stepped into the dining room. He rushed toward her, his cheeks tinged pink from the sun.

"Guess what, Mom? I drove the tractor! I did it all by myself too."

He grinned up at her, and Jacey laughed before she wrapped her arms about his shoulders to give him a quick squeeze. "Really?"

"Sure did," Grant called from across the kitchen. "Kid's a natural. I know who can help me with the plow come fall."

Blaze turned to grin at Grant, and Jacey smiled awkwardly, knowing she and Blaze would only be around for a few more days, a week at most. She wondered what Grant and Helen would do once she and Blaze disappeared. Sooner or later, the Jackmans were bound to discover who she and Blaze really were. Jacey desperately wished she could spare them the pain of her and Melissa's betrayal.

She glanced at Blaze and forced a quick smile. "That's neat,

Blaze. Go wash up now," she instructed quietly as she took her place at the table.

Grant sat opposite her, which placed Kale next to her. She groaned inwardly and again wished that Kale had just gone home. At least with him sitting next to her, she could more easily avoid direct eye contact. His silent appraisals left her feeling weak and vulnerable. It was as if he could read her every thought. She felt more than a little relieved that tonight would be their last encounter. She didn't think she could bear his dour scrutiny much longer.

"Looks delicious, pumpkin." Grant reached over to pinch Helen's plump cheek, and Jacey smiled when Helen swatted his hand away.

"Oh, you," she giggled.

Grant winked at Helen before he addressed Kale, "So, son, you still think Red's going to drop her foal tonight?"

Kale nodded. "I think so. Tonight I hope, but I doubt she'd carry much longer than tomorrow morning. I don't think Red will have much trouble. She's a strong girl."

Grant nodded thoughtfully, glanced at Blaze as the boy joined the adults at the table, then replied, "Well, like I said, I'll stay out at your place tonight. I'll pack a bag after dinner. You just might need some help if she drops tonight. And you're leaving pretty early in the morning—I'll be able to handle it if she holds off till then."

"Just in case, I ought to call Mark. You might need some help in the morning."

Grant nodded his agreement before Helen offered a blessing on the food. The room remained silent, except for the occasional clink of spoons against dishes, as everyone promptly dished up generous portions of Helen's home-cooked food. Jacey's stomach growled as she placed a generous portion of buttered asparagus on her plate, and she smiled when she passed the bowl to Blaze. Blaze grimaced and shook his head before he hurriedly passed the bowl on to Grant.

"Dinner looks great, Mother," Kale commented. He placed a heaping spoonful of mashed potatoes on his plate.

"It does, Aunt Helen," Jacey echoed.

Kale gave her a cursory glance before he passed her the potatoes. She thanked him quietly and spooned a good portion onto her plate. She sighed. She would definitely need to go on one of those terrible "women diets" once she and Blaze moved to the city. Helen's home cooking made portion control nearly impossible.

"Hey, can I come with you and Kale tonight?" Blaze asked Grant.

Jacey quickly shook her head. "No," she told him.

"But I want to see the baby horse too," he responded and glanced toward Uncle Grant for support.

Jacey shook her head again before Grant had a chance to reply, "No, Blaze. I'm sure you'll get to see the baby horse tomorrow."

Blaze sighed and glowered down at his plate of food. " 'S not fair," he mumbled.

Grant laughed loudly. "I'll tell you what, boy. I'll take you out first thing in the morning." He quickly added, "That is, if it's all right with your mother."

"Really?" Blaze perked up and he looked toward Jacey eagerly.

She nodded and gave him a half smile. "That'll be fine."

"I wish I could go tonight, though," Blaze pressed, and Jacey gave him a warning look.

She heard Kale laugh, and she glanced toward him. His eyes twinkled with amusement before he added, "I think your moth- er's right. It's probably best you come out in the morning, Blaze. But I need you to do me a favor." Kale eyed Blaze with a smile.

"What?" Blaze asked.

"I'm not going to be around for the next little while. Every horse needs to have a good name, so why don't you think up a good one for that little foal, and when you see it tomorrow you can give it a name."

Blaze's eyes shone with excitement, and he grinned at Kale, "Really? I get to name him?"

Kale smiled and added, "Well, him or her. You'd better think up a few good girl names too, kid, just in case." Blaze grinned excitedly.

"Cool! Thanks a lot, Kale. I'll pick a real good name."

The atmosphere at dinner seemed much more relaxed than Jacey had thought it would be. Kale's presence wasn't as unbearable as she'd anticipated. Most of the talk around the table involved the farm and animals, and Jacey sat back to listen and enjoy her food.

She would miss Helen's delicious cooking after they left, and she hoped she would have time to cook a little for herself and Blaze once they got settled. She had really enjoyed baking with Helen. She sighed inwardly, then glanced toward Blaze. He'd been unusually quiet throughout the meal, and she watched him carefully before she grinned.

"I think you and I ought to have an early night, babe." She laughed as all eyes turned toward Blaze.

Grant's raucous laughter filled the room when Blaze yawned and mumbled, "I'm all right, Mom."

"You look about ready to face plant in your peas, boy!" Grant slapped Blaze on the back. Blaze grinned sheepishly and yawned again.

"I thought maybe Blaze and I would drive into town tomorrow. Blaze needs some new shoes, and I need a few things as well," Jacey announced quietly.

"I want cowboy boots, Mom, remember? And I want to see the baby horse first," Blaze cut in.

"We'll see," Jacey murmured.

She wondered how expensive cowboy boots were. Their funds were quickly depleting. With the extended drive from Detroit to Utah, the hotels and food, not to mention the price of gas, it had taken a toll on Jacey's hard-earned savings. Once they left the Jackmans, she would need to rely on what she had left to get them by until she found work and received her first paycheck.

"But you said—" Blaze began, and Jacey quickly silenced him with a stern look.

"I said 'we'll see,' Blaze," she warned, and Helen smiled understandingly.

Grant cut in, "Well now, I was thinking about taking you two fishing tomorrow. That is, after your trip into town. What do you think about that, boy? You want to take this old man fishing tomorrow afternoon?"

Blaze visibly brightened, and Jacey couldn't hide her smile.

"Yeah, I would," he exclaimed excitedly. "That would be awesome."

Grant turned toward Jacey. "Sound good to you, darling?"

Jacey's smile broadened and she nodded. "That would be fine." She caught Kale's glance, then added quickly, "That is if it isn't going to keep you from anything."

"Land sakes, honey! Nothing can keep that man from going fishing if he has a mind to do it," Helen interjected, and they all laughed.

"I think that would be a lot of fun, Uncle Grant, but I probably better warn you, Blaze and I have never been fishing before."

She grinned when Grant's eyes widened with mock surprise.

"A couple of greenhorns like you?" He laughed. "Well, I'll tell you, there's nothing to it. We'll stop in at the bait shop and pick up a couple of day licenses. There are several ponds just here in town that should be pretty good to try." He turned to Kale. "You got an extra pole, son?"

Kale nodded. "Out in the shed. I'll pull one out tonight if you'll remind me."

Grant grunted thoughtfully, and Kale suddenly turned to Jacey. He placed his napkin on his empty plate and spoke quietly, "I probably won't see you again before you leave. I'll be gone for a couple of weeks." His chair scraped loudly as he pushed away from the table to stand, "It was good to meet you—*Melissa*."

Jacey couldn't help but wince, and she quickly glanced around at the others to see if they had noticed the change in his tone. Grant and Helen only smiled, but Blaze looked as if he was about to burst into tears. He suddenly jumped from his chair and ran to throw his arms around Kale's waist. Surprised, Kale awkwardly returned the embrace. A smile touched Kale's lips, and he bent to look into Blaze's young face.

"Hey, kid. I'll miss you too." He reached into his shirt pocket and pulled out a small object, then placed it in Blaze's hand. "Here. I found that today, out on the hill behind my house. Do you know what it is?" Kale asked gently.

Blaze opened his hand to examine the small, reddish stone lying in his palm. He shook his head, sniffing loudly.

"That's a real Native American arrowhead. It's made out of red flint. The Ute Indians, when they lived here a long time ago, used to strap these little points to sticks and make arrows. They used these to hunt animals, like rabbits and squirrels. They're pretty hard to find these days." He stood, and Blaze eyed the little point in awe.

"It's real?" he asked, amazed.

"Sure is, kid—genuine artifact. You can take that back to the city and show your friends." Kale laughed, then playfully tapped the end of Blaze's nose.

"Thanks so much. I'll take real good care of it, promise," Blaze responded. Jacey smiled, suddenly grateful to Kale for his gesture. Blaze closed his hand tightly around the small arrowhead and he held it possessively before he sat back in his chair. "I promise I'll pick out a real good name for the baby horse," he announced, "even if it's a girl horse."

Laughter echoed around the room, and Blaze ducked his head shyly before Kale waved to Grant. "I'll see you in a bit, Pops." He kissed Helen swiftly on the cheek. "Thanks for supper, Mother. It was wonderful."

"Be safe, son," Helen called as Kale waved one last time and stepped out.

"Look, Mom," Blaze reached his hand across the table to show Jacey his arrowhead. "Isn't it neat?" His voice filled with pride.

Jacey smiled softly, "It is. That was very nice of Kale to give it to you."

Jacey glanced toward the door, and Helen smiled a little sadly as she made her way back to the table. Jacey sighed inwardly. She wondered about Kale's relationship with his parents. He seemed to be very close to both Helen and Grant, and he had surprised Jacey with his behavior toward Blaze. He seemed to really enjoy having Blaze around. Maybe it was just "Melissa" he didn't like, or maybe it was her. She worried her bottom lip for a short moment. *What does it matter anyway?* she thought angrily. *He'll be gone tomorrow.* There was simply no sense in dwelling on the matter.

She couldn't help but be relieved to see the last of Kale. He confused and worried her. His manner toward her was perplexing, and she was glad not to have to worry about it any longer.

TEN

It was late morning by the time Agents Ronald and Parker pulled up across the street from Melissa McCoy's house. They sat in their unmarked gray sedan and surveyed the house openly.

"Looks like no one's home yet," Parker spoke from the passenger's side.

"Then we wait," Ronald answered, surveying the street.

Parker sat back in his seat with a loud sigh and reached for the bag of Doritos he had purchased when they stopped for gas. He opened the bag and crunched down on a chip.

"Want some?" Parker asked Ronald. He laughed when the older agent glanced at the bag with a scowl.

"No."

"Come on, old man. A couple won't send you into cardiac arrest. Wife got you on a diet?"

Ronald glared, then abruptly leaned over to take a chip. Parker couldn't hold back a grin. The two men sat eating Doritos for a few more minutes before Ronald's cell phone rang. The older man stuffed one last chip in his mouth, chewed quickly, and answered.

"Ronald," he spoke into the phone. Agent Parker checked out the window once more.

He eyed the street carefully. There was still no sign of Melissa McCoy. The surveillance team had said she left from work at ten. It was already nearing noon, and Parker hoped that she hadn't shaken the surveillance team as well.

"Yeah, is that right?" Ronald asked into the phone.

Parker sighed and eyed the homes close by. It seemed like a pretty run-down neighborhood. There was a group of teenaged boys playing a rough game of basketball further away, and Parker could hear their foul language from where he and Ronald sat. Another group of teenagers walked down the road toward them.

The kids eyed Parker and Ronald guardedly as they passed by. Most of the boys were exposing a good six inches of colorful boxers and they had to hold their shorts up as they walked. Parker laughed quietly to himself. He would never understand the new fashions.

"Well?" Parker asked when he realized Ronald had just ended the call. "Did surveillance lose her too?"

"No, she's on her way. Should be here any minute, but we've got ourselves a new situation."

"Oh, yeah, what's that?" Parker queried.

"That was the SAC in the Chicago office. Their agents have it on good authority—from someone on the inside—that Vizcaino or Trent has opened a contract on Jacey Grayson. It looks to me as though Trent's after the boy, and he intends to keep the former Mrs. Trent indefinitely silent."

Parker whistled softly. "Yeah, I'd say that's a new situation. It won't be long before Trent traces Grayson and her boy here, if he hasn't already. She's gone. You don't think Trent got to her already, do you? How long ago was the contract issued?"

Ronald shrugged thoughtfully. "A day or so," he said just as Melissa McCoy's tan Ford Focus pulled into her driveway. "It's possible Trent's got her, but there's only one way to find out." Ronald stepped from the car, and Parker followed. "Come on, sport. Let's get to it," he called over the top of the sedan, and Parker frowned.

"Sure thing, gramps." They stepped across the street and rapidly approached Melissa.

She had gotten out and was bent over, helping her daughter from the back seat. Once she noticed their approach, she stood straight and tensed visibly. The agents pulled out their identification as Ronald addressed her.

"Ms. McCoy, I'm Special Agent Ronald and this is Special Agent Parker," he informed her. "We're with the FBI and we need to ask you a few questions if you don't mind."

Parker watched Melissa McCoy's eyes widen and she turned quickly to her daughter. "Jenny, go into the house, please."

Jenny eyed the two men curiously before she took the keys from her mother. Melissa watched as her daughter crossed the yard and entered the house. Then she turned to face the men. "What can I do for you?" she asked stiffly, her expression guarded.

"We want to talk to you about Jacey Trent, Ms. McCoy," Ronald spoke.

"Jacey Grayson, you mean. She's no longer married to that jerk."

"Excuse me—Jacey Grayson. She was recently living with you, wasn't she, Ms. McCoy?"

Melissa hesitated for a moment, "Yes, she was, but she moved out. She left a few days ago."

Agent Parker took a quick step forward. "Do you mind telling us where she went?" he asked, taking in Melissa McCoy's appearance. She was wearing shorts that showed a good portion of her shapely legs, a sleeveless tank top, and flip flops. Her auburn hair was tied in a loose knot, but her eyes narrowed nervously. Agent Parker couldn't help but like the picture she made. He grinned lazily when she caught his eye.

"Yes, I do." She straightened her back and eyed the two men meaningfully. "I'm sorry," she went on, "but I can't tell you where she went."

"But you do know where she is?" Parker pressed.

"I do," she spoke tightly.

"Ms. McCoy," Ronald addressed her, and she turned anxious eyes toward the older man. "I'm certain you realize that you are under no obligation, at the moment, to tell us what you know, but I feel I must warn you—it's very imperative that we find her."

Parker jumped in hastily, "You see, we've just learned that your friend Jacey Grayson has an open contract out on her, issued by John Trent. Do you understand what that means?"

Melissa's tan face paled visibly, and she grabbed the top of her vehicle for support.

Noticing her strong reaction, Agent Ronald commented gruffly, "I'm certain you understand what that implies."

Melissa remained silent for a long moment before she shook her head. "How do I know this isn't some sort of trick? You know—a 'good cop, bad cop thing' or something?" she questioned. Parker had to smile.

"Ms. McCoy, this is no trick, I can assure you." He leaned toward her, and his eyes met hers firmly. "We have an undercover agent involved. He's deep into the Vizcaino crime gang—our lead is solid. We really do need to know where to find Jacey Grayson and her son, and we need to know before John Trent finds her, if it's not already too late."

Parker knew he'd hit a raw nerve when Miss McCoy's vivid, green eyes filled with tears. "Look, I—well, I just can't tell you guys. Not yet. I need to talk to Jacey. Just give me a day or so to decide what to do." Her voice trembled.

He nodded. "We'll be back soon. If you change your mind before then, call this number. You'll be connected directly to the Detroit Field Office. Again, I feel the need to stress how critical this situation is for Ms. Grayson and her son."

Agent Ronald nodded toward Melissa McCoy before he turned back toward their vehicle.

"We'll see you in a few days, Ms. McCoy," Parker replied before he turned to follow Ronald.

• • •

The little bell on the door jangled as Jacey and Blaze stepped out of the cramped Western wear store. Her eyes narrowed against the sudden brightness outside, and she let the door fall shut with another loud jingle.

"Thanks for the boots, Mom. I can't wait to show these to Uncle Grant and Aunt Helen."

Blaze moved excitedly toward the black Jetta, and Jacey smiled over his obvious excitement. Grant had given her directions to the little shop in Spanish Fork during breakfast. At first Jacey had entered the store warily, but after meeting the kind elderly woman who worked the little shop, Jacey had relaxed.

The lady had shown Blaze and Jacey several pairs of child-sized boots that were within Jacey's price range. It had been fun watching Blaze pick out his first pair of boots. The sales woman had kindly shown him how to pull the boots on, and Jacey had laughed when Blaze took his first unsure steps around the clothes racks. He had grinned and yelled back to her, "These are weird."

"Are you sure you'll be able to walk in them?" Jacey had asked with a broad smile.

The sales woman had laughed and assured he would quickly get used to the feel of his new footwear. Jacey had been slightly pessimistic, but by the time they left the store, Blaze was walking around in the boots with confidence.

"You like them?" Jacey asked as she slipped into the driver's seat.

"I sure do. Now I look like a real cowboy." He placed his hat on his head and beamed at Jacey.

Jacey's smile broadened, "You sure do, Tex." She playfully tipped the edge of his hat as she'd seen Kale do, then started the car.

"Are we going back now?" Blaze asked, rolling down his window to let the stifling heat escape from the car.

"No, not yet. I still need to stop and pick up a newspaper and a few other things before we go back," she replied. "Buckle up, babe."

She heard his belt snap into the lock as she backed the Jetta out of the parking lot and pulled onto the main road. She made her way through town and then turned onto the entrance for the interstate.

"Do you think Red had her baby yet?" Blaze asked anxiously.

Jacey shrugged. "I don't know."

Earlier in the morning, Helen had told them that Southern Red still had not had her foal. Blaze was naturally disappointed, but a quick call from Grant had assured him that he would get to see the baby horse as soon as they got back. Grant felt certain Red was close to having her baby, and Blaze was anxious to get back to the farm. He had spent the entire drive to Spanish Fork sorting through names for a boy or girl horse. He had come up with four names for a boy horse, but had only managed one name for a girl. Jacey had been unable to hide her amusement at Blaze's unwillingness to accept that the new horse could be a girl. He felt certain it would be a boy.

"I can't wait to go fishing today," Blaze commented as he took his hat from off his head and laid it carefully in his lap.

"Neither can I. It'll be fun, I think." Jacey gave him a teasing smile.

She was grateful Blaze was getting the opportunities they were experiencing with Grant and Helen. Fishing was something she would never have been able to do with Blaze by herself. Jacey sighed as her mind shifted to their future. She hoped a newspaper would provide a bit of information on job opportunities in Salt Lake. In a few days, she and Blaze would need to be on their way. She was anxious to begin a new life, yet she felt reluctant to leave.

More and more, she was finding it easier to slip into life as Melissa. She enjoyed Helen and Grant's company. She loved feeling as though she was part of a family again. It was a feeling she hadn't experienced since she'd lost her own parents. She shook her head slightly and tried to focus on the plans she had hastily put together the night before.

Jacey had decided that she and Blaze would travel to Salt Lake in a few days. They would stay in a hotel until she could find a cheap apartment, and she desperately hoped it would only take a few days to find a suitable place to live. She planned on looking for work over the next couple of days while they finished their stay with Helen and Grant. Jacey knew she could find plenty of time to slip away during the day to call about the openings, and she hoped she could convince people to conduct interviews over the phone.

ELEVEN

Melissa watched with fearful eyes as the two agents returned to their vehicle. Her legs felt weak, and she grasped the top of her car for support. She sighed with relief when the agents' car pulled away from the curb and drove slowly out of sight.

"Oh, girl, you're in a mess," she whispered into the silent heat as she turned and made her way inside. She shut the door and jumped slightly when she caught sight of Jenny moving away from the front window.

"Who were those men?" Jenny asked suspiciously.

Melissa shook her head. "Just a couple of guys. They needed to ask me a few questions." She caught Jenny's worried eye and forced a quick smile. "Don't worry about it, kiddo. Hey, do you think you could bring me the phone, toots?"

Jenny nodded solemnly and turned toward the kitchen. Melissa sank gratefully onto her worn sofa. She forced a smile when Jenny returned with her cell phone. "Thanks, babe," she said. Then she added, "Why don't you go upstairs? You can watch the tube in your room for a bit."

Jenny's eyebrows rose questioningly. "I don't have to do chores first?" she asked. "Are you feeling all right?" Jenny attempted to tease.

Melissa gave her a quick half smile. "Get upstairs, twerp—before I change my mind."

Jenny smiled and shrugged. "All right, I won't argue."

Melissa listened as Jenny padded into the kitchen. She heard the snack cupboard door creak and the unmistakable rustle of the chip bag. The cupboard door shut, and the sound of Jenny's stocking feet receded upstairs. Melissa reached a trembling hand toward the phone and took a deep breath. She dialed Jacey's familiar cell phone number and waited breathlessly as the phones connected.

"No," she whispered anxiously when the phone went straight to Jacey's voice mail. She immediately redialed. "Come on, girl, pick up."

The phone took another moment to reconnect, and Melissa cursed when it kicked her directly to voice mail once again. She tapped her newly polished nails nervously against her teeth as she waited for Jacey's voice mail introduction. At the beep she took a deep breath and spoke quickly, "I need to talk to you, babe. It's important. Call me right away. Love you, girl. Bye."

Melissa sighed noisily as she slammed her body against the soft cushions of the sofa. The sound of the steady clock seemed exaggerated in the silence of the living room, and she could hear the muffled sounds of Jenny's television upstairs. She groaned quietly, then decidedly pushed herself up from the couch and entered the kitchen.

"Where did I put it?" she grumbled, searching her file drawer in the kitchen. "There you are," Melissa breathed a moment later when she pulled a folded sheet of paper from the bottom of the drawer.

She flipped it open and eyed the Jackman's phone number and address anxiously. Should she call them directly? Melissa worried that she would mess up and give Jacey away, but what if Jacey had never made it to Utah in the first place?

With her mind made up, she tossed the paper onto the kitchen table, flipped the phone open, and dialed the number. She held her breath as Grant and Helen's home phone rang.

"Hello?" she heard Helen's vaguely familiar voice answer after six rings.

Melissa took a rushed, calming breath before she spoke into the phone. "Hi, I'm a friend of—" she paused momentarily, then hurriedly added, "Melissa McCoy's. I was wondering, is she there?" Melissa held her breath, waiting to hear the worst.

"Oh, dear—" Helen's voice called over the line, and Melissa's teeth clenched tightly. "No, no, she's not here at the moment."

"She—she's not?" Melissa grasped the back of a kitchen chair. "I—"

"Melissa and Blaze drove into town this morning," Helen continued, "but she should be back any time."

She's there, she thought with sudden relief. Melissa's body relaxed, and she gave a shaky laugh into the phone. "Oh, then— she'll be back soon?" she asked.

"She should be, dear. Why don't you leave your name and number and I'll have her give you a ring as soon as she gets in," Helen suggested kindly.

"Thank you," Melissa breathed. "Tell her that Jacey from Detroit called. I need her to call me as soon as she can. It's really important."

"I will certainly have her call you, dear. Do you want to leave your number?" Helen responded.

"No, she has my number. Will you just have her call me? That would be great."

"I'll see that she gets the message. Thank you," Helen replied. "Good-bye."

"Bye, and thank you," Melissa added before the line went silent.

Thank goodness Jacey made it safely to Utah. She hoped Jacey and Blaze wouldn't take much longer in town. Melissa shook her head with relief as she stepped to her old refrigerator. She opened its vintage door and let the cold air rush onto her flushed face. She reached for a soda just as she heard Jenny's voice from upstairs.

"Mom," Jenny called, and Melissa paused at the unfamiliar note in her daughter's voice.

"Jenny? What is it, toots?" She shut the fridge door, took another gulp of soda, stepped toward the stairs, and looked up curiously. Jenny screamed suddenly and Melissa jumped, banging her elbow hard against the railing. Loud, pounding steps rattled the upstairs floor.

"Jenny!" The soda dropped from Melissa's hand, and she made a mad dash up the stairs. "Jenny!" she screamed as she reached the landing.

She turned into the hall that led to Jenny's bedroom and abruptly froze when John Trent's sneering gaze met hers over the top of her daughter's head. He took a step forward, forcing Jenny to move with him. He grasped the little girl's hair tightly in one hand and held a small handgun firmly in the other. Time seemed to move in slow motion as Melissa's mind registered all that was happening. She felt the blood rush from her head as she faced the fear in her daughter's eyes.

"Jenny, no," Melissa choked. Her blood ran cold. "Let her go!" she ground out through tightly clenched teeth.

Melissa reached a hand toward Jenny, and she took a staggering step forward. John tugged harder against the girl's ponytail, and Jenny whimpered. Silent tears spilled down her pale face.

"What is this? No 'Hi, how are you?' or 'Good to see you' or 'It's been a long time, John?'" John sneered. He shook his head, smiling slowly. "You never did have any manners."

"Let my daughter go!" Melissa screamed angrily.

"We need to talk first." John's face grew suddenly serious, and Melissa jumped when another man appeared behind John. He smiled casually and ran a deeply tanned hand across his short, black hair.

"Who are you?" Melissa asked heatedly. "What do you want?"

"Downstairs. We'll talk." John cocked his head toward the stairs and sneered, "Ladies first."

Melissa stood frozen for a moment before she turned and stepped onto the first step. She grasped the railing tightly in order to support her trembling legs as she descended the steep staircase. She kept Jenny in her peripheral sight and gritted her teeth as John pushed her little girl ahead of him and descended the stairs. The stranger followed John silently.

She reached the bottom and turned into the kitchen before she spun around to face John angrily. "Let her go! Now!"

John shook his head. "You're looking good, Melissa." His eyes ran the length of her body, and he smiled cruelly. His gaze rested on the length of her bare legs, exposed below her shorts.

"What do you want?" she demanded loudly. "If you're look-ing for Jacey and Blaze, then they're gone, all right?"

"So I heard," John said derisively. "Where'd she go? Where's *Melissa*?"

Melissa paled, realizing he must have heard her conversation with Helen. He must have heard her ask for Melissa instead of Jacey. She shuddered visibly before her eyes fell automatically to the paper she had left on the kitchen table. John laughed as he followed her gaze. He pushed Jenny ahead a step, then reached around her rigid form to grasp the paper.

His eyes flicked over the information casually before his gaze shot back toward Melissa, "You've been a big help, Melissa."

"Let my daughter go," Melissa commanded in a strained voice.

John laughed cruelly before he abruptly let Jenny go. Jenny gasped when she fell to the floor, and Melissa rushed to her daugh-ter's side. She gathered Jenny tightly against her, then bolted away from John. She held Jenny's face against her chest as the little girl sobbed uncontrollably.

Melissa glared openly. "Get out!" she screamed.

John laughed. "Take care of them." He turned to face the stranger who stood behind him, then tossed him an envelope and grinned. "Make some trunk music."

The stranger leered at Melissa. "No problem."

John placed his revolver back inside his sport coat and, with-out another glance toward Melissa or Jenny, he stepped toward the patio doors and disappeared outside.

• • •

It had been a nice trip into town, but Jacey was amazed at how great it felt to be back. Her mind fleetingly conjured the word "home," and Jacey shook her head, frustrated. The Jackman's place did feel like home, but she and Blaze didn't belong there. *In fact*, she thought guiltily, *we shouldn't even be here.* She sighed as she shifted the car into park and pushed her troubling thoughts away. She reached into the backseat to retrieve their purchases.

Excited to show off his new boots, Blaze bolted from the car and made a hasty, wobbling effort to cross the gravel drive. Jacey hid a smile as he reached the porch and stumbled on the stairs.

"Are you all right?" she called out to him.

"Uh-huh," he replied as he crossed the porch and disappeared inside the house.

Jacey shook her head and smiled. She hoped Blaze didn't break a leg before he got used to his new boots. Her feet crunched on the hot gravel, and she slowly made her way toward the house. She savored the feeling of stepping into the cool shade of the Jackman's covered porch. A slight breeze teased her hair. She brushed the wisps of long hair from her face and turned to gaze out across the fields toward the high peaks of Mt. Nebo.

Grant had mentioned taking a trip to see "the loop," and Jacey wondered if they would get a chance to visit the magnificent-looking mountains before she and Blaze had to leave. She sighed. She would desperately miss the beauty of the Jackman's home.

As Jacey entered the house, she was met with an unusual silence. She placed her bags on the table and glanced around curiously, wondering where Helen was. Blaze's muffled voice drifted in from outside, and Jacey knew he must have gone to find Grant or visit his horse. She stepped to the kitchen sink and ran herself a cool glass of water. She gulped thirstily before deciding to join Blaze outside.

As she stepped through the mudroom, she was surprised to hear Blaze's voice coming from across the opposite side of the yard, rather than near corrals. She turned curiously toward the sound and smiled when she found Helen on her knees, pulling weeds in a sunny patch of garden. Blaze sat cross-legged in the long, cool grass, and he waved as Jacey approached. Helen turned and gave Jacey an awkward wave.

"Hi, dear," she called.

"Mom." Blaze jumped up quickly. He wobbled unsteadily for a moment before he rushed toward her. "Southern Red had her baby! Can we go see it?"

He grasped her arm excitedly, and Jacey laughed. Helen groaned and pushed herself to stand. She gave herself a quick brush-off and pulled her muddy-fingered gloves off her hands.

"That's right." She smiled kindly into Jacey's eyes. "Uncle

Grant and Kale delivered the little thing just two hours ago."

"Really?" Jacey asked, startled. She was sure Kale had mentioned he would have to leave early in the morning. It was already mid-afternoon. "Is Kale still here?" she queried uncertainly.

Helen grinned and nodded.

"So can we go, Mom?" Blaze jumped in as Jacey frowned.

"I don't know, son," she murmured. She raised a hand to her fluttering stomach and quickly tried to mask her sudden anxiety.

"Kale got a call early this morning," Helen informed her. "The company he works for said they didn't need him to go on this trip after all, since their proposal to open the new drill site was shot down by the Public Lands Council. So he won't need to go again for at least another week or so."

"Mom, I want to see the baby horse," Blaze begged.

"Later, babe." Jacey grasped his shoulder and gave it a quick squeeze. Blaze scowled down at the grass as he and Jacey followed Helen into the coolness of the house.

Helen gave Blaze an encouraging smile. "Uncle Grant and Kale should be back here anytime, dear. I'm sure when they get here, Kale will run you out to see the colt."

Blaze nodded unhappily, and Jacey gave him an exaggerated look just as Helen offered, "Why don't you sit and have one of my muffins."

"I guess," Blaze grumbled.

Helen winked at Jacey before she added, "They're my famous chocolate chip muffins."

Blaze gave Helen a faint smile. "Kay," he mumbled, slumping into a chair.

Jacey and Helen shared a quick, knowing look before Jacey commented, "I bought a few groceries. I would have put them away already, but I'm not certain where you want them." She grasped the plastic sacks off the table and carried them into the kitchen.

"Well, goodness, you didn't need to do that, Melissa."

Jacey smiled into the older woman's kind eyes. "It's the least I could do," she said, laughing. "It isn't much."

"Well, thank you, dear." Helen gave Jacey a quick hug. "Oh, and here comes Kale."

Helen winked at Jacey when Blaze bolted from the table and rushed to the door to watch as Kale drove Grant's truck into the driveway. A few short moments passed before Kale stepped into the house, and Blaze backed up with a quick smile to let him enter.

Kale winked as he stepped in. "Hey there, kid."

"Hi, Kale! Is the baby horse okay? I want to go and see it, but Mom won't take me," Blaze accused.

"She won't, huh?" Kale glanced quickly at Jacey, and she forced a smile.

"How's the colt?" Helen asked promptly.

Kale grinned, and his eyes shone excitedly. "It's a good-looking horse, strong too."

Jacey turned away from the others. She tried to focus on placing the meager groceries she had purchased into the cupboards.

"How did Red handle it?" Helen asked.

Kale walked toward the sink, and his shoulder brushed Jacey's. Instinctively, she stepped away. She held her breath and listened, curious.

"She did great. We didn't have to help her much," Kale answered.

He flipped the water on and washed his hands. With his back to her, Jacey quickly took in his appearance. There was a small hole in his left sock where the end of his big toe protruded. His face was unshaven, and she could see the ring around his head where his hat had pressed his hair flat. She suddenly couldn't help but think that he was an extremely handsome man. Her heart gave a quick lurch, and she turned away, frustrated at her wandering thoughts. That man affected her in more ways than one, and Jacey silently cursed the Public Land Council or whatever it was that had prevented Kale's trip.

She sighed inwardly before she grabbed a box of cereal off the counter, then stood on tip toes to reach the high shelf where Helen stored the dry cereal. She groaned quietly and stretched her arm high just as she suddenly felt Kale's large body move behind hers. Jacey froze when Kale's hard chest brushed against her back, and his hand came up to take the box of cereal from her. His free hand suddenly cupped her thin shoulder, and he placed the box easily onto the high shelf. Jacey held her breath tightly and tried to still the unexpected rush of butterflies racing about in the pit of her stomach. He stepped away, but the warmth of his hand lingered.

"Thank you." Jacey's voice sounded breathless to her own ears, and she groaned internally. Kale eyed her with a strange mixed expression before he nodded and turned toward the table.

"Hey, kid, hand over a muffin," he growled playfully to Blaze, and Jacey heard her son giggle.

She turned and watched as Blaze pushed the plate toward Kale. Kale reached for the butter, and steam rose in tiny, snake-like tendrils from the soft muffin as Kale broke it open to smear a generous slab of butter on it. Jacey suppressed a sudden longing to feel the warmth of his hand on her shoulder again.

"Oh dear, Melissa," Helen said suddenly, and Jacey turned, startled.

A deep blush rose to her cheeks, and she hoped Helen hadn't noticed her watching Kale. *What on earth am I thinking?* she silently berated herself.

Helen looked suddenly flustered, and Jacey asked quickly, "What is it?"

"I nearly forgot. A friend of yours from Detroit phoned earlier. She said it was important. I'm so sorry. I should have told you as soon as you got home." Helen looked apologetic, and Jacey's heart suddenly jumped.

"Who was it?" she asked.

Had John found her? She and Melissa had agreed not to contact one another until she and Blaze had moved to Salt Lake.

Helen paused for a thoughtful moment before she replied, "Her name was . . . Jacey! That's it. She said you had her number."

Jacey paled suddenly. Why would Melissa try calling her here, through Helen and Grant's direct number?

"I'll—I'll go and call her back." Jacey forced a quick smile before she rushed upstairs.

Her heart was pounding nervously as she located the cell phone she had purposely left in the top dresser drawer. She waited impatiently as the phone turned on, and immediately Jacey noticed that she had missed two calls from Melissa, back to back. Her heart thudded as she hit redial and waited for the phone to connect. Then she sat with bated breath as Melissa's phone rang several times before sending her call to voice mail.

"No," she breathed and dialed again. "Melissa, what's going on?"

When there was still no answer, Jacey closed her phone. She took a deep breath and placed it in her pocket. *Everything is fine. She was just calling to check on us,* Jacey tried to reassure herself. She shook her head and stood to gaze at her pale reflection in the mirror.

"You're overreacting," she whispered to the wide eyes staring back at her. Jacey sighed and rubbed the back of her neck before she opened her door and slowly made her way back downstairs. As Jacey stepped into the dining room, she caught Kale's eye and forced a smile. She cast a quick look at Blaze and paused when she saw the unmasked panic in his expression.

"What is it, Mom?"

Jacey shook her head, faking a smile. "Nothing, Blaze. Jacey just wanted to talk, that's all. She wanted to see how we were doing."

Kale turned to watch Blaze, and Jacey gave her son a quick warning glance over the top of Kale's head. She hoped Blaze's sudden fear or her worried reaction hadn't been noticeable to the Jackmans. Kale's attention returned to Jacey, and again she gave him her best forced smile as she walked past him into the kitchen.

"Did you get in touch with your friend, dear?" Helen asked.

"Yes, she just needed to know when I'd be back to work." Her stomach turned. She hated lying to Helen, yet the lies came so easily. *But isn't that what this is?* Jacey thought silently. *Isn't it all just a lie?* She sighed as she ran herself another cold glass of water and gulped it down. She and Blaze needed to get out of this place. She didn't know if she could handle the oppressive guilt for much longer. The more time they spent with Grant and Helen, the harder it would be to conceal the truth.

"Blaze?" Kale's voice caused Jacey to turn. "If it's all right with your mom," he paused and glanced at Jacey, "maybe you could ride back to my place to see that colt while I scrounge up a couple fishing poles?"

Blaze seemed to relax. He nodded. "Yeah, sure. Can I, Mom?"

Jacey smiled and nodded her agreement. "That would be fine." Then she added, "But make sure you mind Kale."

Blaze scowled. "I will, Mom, jeez."

"He'll be fine," Kale said, before turning to face Helen. "Dad and I should be ready to go within the hour."

Helen gave a little wave. "I'll pack you four a picnic, but I think I'll stay behind and do a bit of baking, if that's all right." She glanced at Jacey.

"Oh, that's fine, Aunt Helen," Jacey hastened to reassure her.

"I'd love to go, but I never did take to fishing, and Sister Theo, she lives in town, has terrible bouts of arthritis. She's just had an awful time lately. I was thinking I'd like to make a pot of stew and a couple loaves of bread to take over," she explained. Then she asked Blaze, "What name did you decide on, dear, for that little horse?"

Blaze looked thoughtful for a moment before he smiled, "I'm going to have to see him first. I'm glad he's not a girl 'cause I don't like picking out girl names."

Kale and Helen chuckled, and Blaze grinned sheepishly. "I'm probably going to name him Avatar. Or Uncle Grant liked Trigger."

"Avatar?" Jacey asked with a smile. "Isn't that the cartoon you always watch?"

"Uh-huh. *Avatar*'s awesome."

"Avatar, huh?" Kale chuckled. "I kinda like that one."

Blaze nodded. "Me too, but I might name him Trigger, 'cause that was Uncle Grant's favorite."

"That man!" Helen interjected. "If Uncle Grant had his way, he'd name every horse on this farm Trigger."

They all laughed. Then Kale said, "Come on, kid. Let's go see if that colt looks like a Trigger or an Avatar."

Jacey could still hear Kale's deep laughter as he and Blaze stepped out into the yard, and she smiled to herself. It was a nice change to see Kale smiling instead of scowling.

"Why don't you sit down and rest for a bit? Have a muffin," Helen suggested, and Jacey obliged willing.

The smell of Helen's fresh muffins had been tempting Jacey

ever since Helen had first offered them to Blaze. She joined Helen at the table and buttered a warm muffin.

"Did you have a good time in town, dear?" Helen asked. "Blaze looks so handsome in his new boots. He was so proud when he showed them to me a little earlier."

Jacey smiled softly. "We had a good time, and we enjoyed the drive. The mountains seemed so close at times. It's really very beautiful here."

"It is, isn't it? Grant and I have been happy here. It's grown the past several years, but we still enjoy it."

Jacey bit into her muffin and let her gaze wander toward the wide window. She could see a trail of dust coming off the lane leading to Kale's property, and she wondered what Blaze would think of the colt. She would have liked to have gone along to see his reaction. She sighed as she took another delectable bite of her muffin and let her mind wander over Blaze's reaction to Melissa's call.

Even as he had left with Kale, Jacey had detected a strain around Blaze's young mouth, and his eyes had seemed haunted. Why had a phone call from Melissa caused such a deep reaction in a nine-year-old boy? Maybe he had been worried it would be John. That had been her first thought. Jacey sighed and stared, unseeing, out the window. She couldn't help but feel something terrible had happened between Blaze and his father before the divorce. What had John done to frighten Blaze so badly? Jacey closed her eyes for a moment. She suddenly felt overwhelmed.

"Melissa," Helen's voice jumped into Jacey's thoughts.

"Yes?" she asked with tight smile.

"Are you all right, dear?"

Helen eyed her with motherly concern, and Jacey's mouth quivered slightly. She suddenly wanted to throw herself into Helen's plump arms and tell her everything, but she nodded stiffly instead.

"I'm fine. I was just . . . thinking." Jacey forced a laugh.

"Well, if there's anything you ever want to talk about, I'm always here to listen." Helen reached across and clasped Jacey's hand.

Jacey responded with a shaky smile. "Thank you, Aunt Helen." She squeezed Helen's warm, soft hand gently. "That means a lot."

TWELVE

John laughed, pleased with himself, as he opened the passenger door of Rafael's black Mercedes. Rafael scowled knowingly but remained silent as John entered the vehicle.

"Looks like I need to go west," John sneered as he pulled the folded paper from his pocket and eyed the Utah address carefully.

Rafael rolled his eyes, then asked gruffly, "Your old lady's not around?"

John shook his head as he pulled a cigarette from the inside of his jacket. He lit the end and took a long drag. "No." Tendrils of smoke snaked out from around the corners of his mouth. "Stupid broad took my boy and ran to Utah."

"Oh yeah? What's in Utah?" Rafael asked with narrowed eyes.

John shrugged and laughed. "Sand?" he mocked. "How should I know?" He took another drag. "She's pretending to be that stupid broad, Melissa. Jacey always did have peanuts for brains. Did she think that a mindless trick like that would keep me from finding her?" He laughed.

Rafael glared openly. Throwing his hands up derisively, he asked, "So you think you need to go to Utah now, John?"

"Hey," John scowled at his partner, "I want my boy back. You got a problem with that, Ralph?"

Rafael shook his head, frustrated, and raised a hand to rub his thick goatee. "Johnny, the boss ain't gonna like this. I saw a couple of badges talkin' to that lady. Your son's gone and ratted. Bringing that boy on the job was a bad idea. If they find that reporter's body . . . . The Fed's tie us to that job—they could shut our whole outfit down. They're gonna clip you good, Johnny."

John took a deep breath. He could feel his temper rise. He took another drag on the cigarette and ground out slowly, "My boy ain't no rat. Like I told you, he's my made-man."

Rafael laughed loudly. "Made-man? What are you, thick in the head? He's a kid, John!" He threw his hands in the air, exasperated, and sighed heavily. "Listen John, administration says the books are open. That could mean big bucks for this thing of ours. Think about it, Johnny."

John shook his head angrily and eyed Rafael. *What did he know, anyway?* "I want my kid, Ralph. Take me to the airport."

"You been listening to me? I said the books are open! Let the woman go. Get you another broad," Rafael returned angrily as he started the Mercedes.

Rafael shook his head as he slammed the vehicle into gear and drove through the crowded streets. John remained silent. His eyes were fixed on the passing neighborhood.

"Listen Johnny," Rafael began more calmly. "This Sal—he's a wise guy. I've got this gut feeling about him, you know. He's *potzo*—crazy! We've got work to do. The street crew's been busy with new shipments and—"

"This thing of ours can wait!" John cut him off sharply.

Rafael slammed the palm of his hands against the steering wheel, frustrated. "All right, forget it. I take you as far as Wayne County, then you're on your own! When the boss finds out, you're a dead man, Johnny." Rafael glanced angrily toward John, then spit scornfully out the window. When John's eyes remained fixed ahead, Rafael sighed, shaking his head, "*Che peccato*—your throat."

• • •

"How many ponds are there?" Jacey asked Grant curiously.

She gazed across the small pond with wonder. Tall grass and dusty Russian olive trees touched blue sky, and various bird songs sounded all around them.

"A few," Grant answered. "Three or four."

Jacey nodded thoughtfully and leaned toward the edge of the pond to peer through the perfectly clear water. She could see the bottom, and she watched in amazement as another small crayfish scuttled across the moss-strewn silt.

"I saw another crayfish," she called out to Blaze.

Blaze gave her a fleeting look before he turned back toward his pole. He exhaled noisily, then asked, uninterested, "Is it still there?"

She turned back toward the water and searched its shallow depths for a short moment. "No, it must have moved into the moss."

Blaze scowled, staring out across the pond. Jacey hid a smile. She couldn't help but feel amused as she watched her son. They had been fishing for only an hour at best. Blaze had expected to catch a fish right off, but so far, no one had even had a nibble.

She laughed quietly to herself and watched with fascination as another funny-looking duck bobbed along the calm water. Its odd-shaped head moved forward and back, reminding her of an old-fashioned pull toy. She felt amazed by the little wetland hidden just outside of town. It was like being at a zoo. So far they had seen a heron flying in the distance, every breed of duck imaginable, and Blaze had even found a water snake slithering through the tall grass along the edge of the pond.

Jacey grimaced inwardly at the thought of the slinky little snake before she gave the area around her a quick inspection. She hadn't been impressed with the snake. She glanced toward her pole and wondered if she shouldn't reel in again and try casting her line further out, but she quickly quelled the idea. She still didn't have the whole casting bit down. Her line had ended up tangled in the nearby bushes twice already, and she wasn't sure she wanted to risk the same mishap again.

Blaze had caught on quickly to casting, and after the first few tries, he had become quite the little sportsman. Every now and again, Jacey would catch him reeling in his pole to check on his worm before casting out again. Kale had spent nearly twenty minutes helping Blaze learn to cast and teaching him how to bait his hook. Jacey was impressed with Kale's patience with her son.

Thankfully, Uncle Grant had not made good on his promise to make everyone bait their own hook, and he had happily placed a wiggly worm on Jacey's hook. She had watched with mixed feelings of disgust and amazement as he threaded the fat, slimy creature onto the sharp point.

Kale had caught her eye during the ordeal to give her a quick mocking smile, but she had promptly turned away from his accusing eyes. After leaving the ranch, he had quickly reverted back to his gruff attitude toward her, and he'd said little to her since they arrived at the ponds.

She glanced toward Kale. He sat to her left, his back propped up by a smooth boulder, his long legs stretched out comfortably in the tall grass, and his hat over his eyes. Jacey wondered if he was asleep. He hadn't said a word since he'd cast his line into the water. She then turned her attention to Blaze and watched with amusement as her son stood to reel in his line. He scowled, evidently disgusted, when he saw his soggy worm still hanging from his hook.

"Won't catch a fish with your pole out of the water, boy," Grant called laughingly.

Jacey smiled, turning back toward her pole.

"How long do you have to wait?" Blaze asked impatiently. He tapped his limp worm with the tip of his finger. "I think my worm's dead," he moaned.

Grant laughed loudly. Standing, he stretched his thick shoulders. "Why don't you and I head over to the next pond? We'll try a spinner over there where the water's a bit deeper," Grant offered good-naturedly.

Blaze's expression instantly rose, and he asked eagerly, "What's a spinner?"

"Well, let's get on over there, and I'll show you." The older man chuckled and turned to Jacey. "You and Kale stay put. We won't be gone long."

Suddenly unsure, Jacey glanced at Kale. She noticed he had sat up and was looking at her with a strange expression. She turned to Blaze and Grant, "I—well—"

Blaze grinned, and Grant sent a quick wink her way. "We'll be back soon."

"Bye, Mom." Blaze waved as he grabbed his pole and followed Grant.

"Bye," she returned. Then she pushed her attention back to her pole.

Ignoring Kale, Jacey glanced out across the pond and gasped quietly when she caught sight of a graceful heron standing against the opposite bank, directly in front of her. She watched with wide-eyed amazement as the graceful bird gave her a measuring look. Deciding all was safe, it dipped its gray head down into the shallow water.

"There's a pair of herons that nest over there in those Russian olive trees. You can see the nest through the branches if you look real close," Kale spoke in a hushed tone.

Jacey turned surprised eyes toward his. "Really?" she whispered, amazed that Kale would tell her something like that. Everything he had said to her since leaving the farm earlier had been clipped and strained, and now this? Her eyes narrowed hesitantly, and she felt confused by his ever-changing attitude toward her. She squinted in the direction Kale had indicated but couldn't see the nest in the trees' thick foliage. She gave up and turned her attention back to the bird.

"They're beautiful. They look so graceful," Jacey whispered.

The bird suddenly tensed and looked their way.

Kale nodded and slowly reached for his pole to reel in. "I used to come here as a boy. I spent a lot of time fishing. There's a lot of wildlife out here. If you're lucky, you can sometimes see an otter or two toward evening."

"These ponds are remarkable, really. The water is so clear, and I've never seen a crayfish until today. Well, at least one that's still alive. I've seen several just since we've been here. They scuttle along the bottom. It's amazing," Jacey commented in hushed tones.

Kale nodded and gave her a half smile. "If you can catch them, they're pretty good eating. They're fast little suckers though."

"They look just like baby lobsters." Jacey chuckled softly, and Kale nodded with a slight smile.

He didn't comment but turned his attention back toward the pond, and Jacey squirmed in the sudden silence that stretched between them. She sighed in disappointment, then glanced anxiously at her pole. It hadn't even twitched. She wondered if she should reel in and go look for Blaze and Grant.

Suddenly Kale stood. The heron splashed loudly, and Jacey jumped a little as the large bird quickly darted for open sky. She could hear the soft whisper of its giant wings as it caught the air and disappeared behind a wall of trees and brush. Her shoulders sagged, and she turned to face Kale with accusing eyes. He glared toward the water for a short moment before he abruptly moved over to sit on the boulder closest to her. Jacey's mouth went dry as he faced her with a determined expression.

"Listen, you and I—we need to talk," he spoke gruffly, and Jacey's eyes widened warily.

"What about, Kale?" she asked slowly, her stomach churning. She glanced down at the long grass near her legs, took a deep breath, and met his eyes questioningly.

"A few years back I took a business trip. I had to go to Chicago," Kale began gruffly.

Jacey swallowed, and he continued. His gaze was startlingly direct. "My trip happened to be right after Uncle James died. When Pops found out that his brother had died and he hadn't been told until days after the funeral, it nearly broke the old man's heart. So . . ." Kale paused.

Jacey anxiously brought a trembling hand to the middle of her stomach. Her eyes widened with ever-increasing concern.

"So I went to find Melissa and her family while I was out there." Kale's eyes narrowed as he watched Jacey's face grow pale. "I found Melissa, but I never did approach her or her family. I was still too angry. I didn't trust myself to meet them, but I saw Melissa."

He knows. Jacey shut her eyes for a quick, stomach-turning moment, then raised fearful eyes to meet his. She felt as if she would faint when he finished brusquely, "And you are not Melissa."

Jacey's eyes widened, and she whispered almost inaudibly. "But why?" Her eyes narrowed incredulously. "You've known this whole time and—" She paused to take a shaky breath.

Kale's firm expression remained fixed on her as she continued in a small, trembling voice, "Does Uncle Grant—? Does he—?"

127

She stopped and shook her head, feeling terribly overwhelmed.

"Does Dad know?" Kale finished for her. "No, as far as I know, he doesn't. I have the feeling he's a bit suspicious, but he hasn't said anything, and I haven't told him anything—that is, at least, not yet."

Jacey immediately felt less anxious and turned pleading eyes toward his. How was she going to explain?

"Are you going to tell him? And—well, why haven't you said anything?" she asked quietly.

She glanced toward the narrow dirt lane at the spot where Grant and Blaze had disappeared. She bit her bottom lip nervously before her gaze found Kale's. Her eyes were wide and anxious.

Kale's eyes narrowed slightly as they fell on her mouth. Jacey held her breath. He shook his head and blew out a long, slow breath as he removed his battered hat. Wiping an arm across his forehead, he turned and stared out toward the pond. "I figured you must have a pretty good reason to come out here pretending to be someone you're not. So," he looked at her suddenly, his expression unreadable, "who are you? And why are you here?"

Jacey breathed deeply, clamping her sweaty hands together. Her hands were trembling visibly. She took another deep breath before she attempted to explain. "I was worried. I—well, my ex-husband . . . . You see, I was worried he was going to try to take Blaze from me. So I had to hide. I needed to go somewhere safe, somewhere he wouldn't think to look for me." She stopped and watched Kale carefully.

He groaned and shook his head with obvious agitation. "So why are you here? Why pretend to be Melissa? And who are you?" he demanded slowly, his expression growing more annoyed.

Jacey cringed. Her heart thumped madly in her chest, and she watched him closely as she went on, "My name is Jacey—Jacey Grayson. I'm sorry, Kale, but Melissa is my best friend. We were living together, but I had to leave. I had to have a different name. John—he could trace Blaze and me no matter where we went. Melissa thought that if I went as 'Melissa' to her relatives, it would strengthen my cover until I could come up with a more permanent idea to stay hidden from John," she finished breathlessly.

Kale eyed her silently for what seemed like an endless minute. "So you created an alias," he stated. His eyes narrowed angrily. "Why go through with it then? Why not create the story, then disappear? You could have disappeared as Melissa to anywhere in the country. Why did you come here?"

Jacey sighed, feeling more deflated by the minute. "Please try to understand, Kale. I needed a place to stay. I couldn't stay with Melissa anymore. I don't have any family of my own—well, at least not any that would be willing to help—and besides, that would be the first place John would look. I couldn't take my son and disappear without a safe place to go. I have to find a job and a place to live. A hotel would have depleted my funds too quickly, and John—" Jacey paused when Kale suddenly stood and walked to the edge of the pond.

He stared out across the water and rubbed a hand absently against the back of his neck before he turned to glare at her. "Lady, there are other ways to protect Blaze from your ex-husband. There are ways that don't involve dragging—*using*—my parents."

How do I explain? Jacey wondered. Tears blurred her vision and she looked down, ashamed, as a fat tear rolled off her cheek.

"Kale, I'm sorry," she whispered. "Truly I am. I never meant to use them." She looked up to meet his gaze. "I love Grant and Helen, as if they truly were my family. No one has ever been kinder to me. I don't want to hurt them. It was never my intention, please believe me. But John—"

Kale moved to sit on the rock. His expression looked troubled and their eyes met briefly. She shook her head and glanced down toward the ground.

"But John what?" he asked brusquely. "Why is it so important that you hide from your ex-husband? There are other ways to protect Blaze."

Jacey rubbed a trembling hand across the tears spilling down her cheek. She shook her head wearily. "It's hard to explain," she began quietly.

"Try," Kale interjected. "I think I deserve an explanation—a very thorough explanation. Why don't you start with why you left him?"

Jacey looked up apprehensively. Kale's gaze remained firm, and she sighed resolutely.

"John," she shrugged, "John is a very, well, temperamental man. He—when we were married—when he'd get angry, really angry, he'd get violent. Sometimes very violent," she said softly. "He never hit Blaze, but I hated Blaze seeing John hit me as often as he did."

"How long were you married?" Kale jumped in, his expression softer.

"A little over eight years," she answered. "I left him six months ago. Everyone always asks me why I stayed so long, but—it's so difficult to explain."

"Why *did* you?"

Jacey shook her head and sighed. "Sometimes I don't really understand myself, but I think I stayed because I always hoped he would change, and well, mostly because I was scared. I had been with John for so long. I married so young. John is quite a bit older than me, and I didn't believe I could make it on my own. John always reminded me that I never could. He threatened to take Blaze from me if I ever left. He promised I would never see my son again so—so, I stayed."

"What happened to finally make you leave?" Kale asked, watching Jacey closely.

Her eyes met his, and she swallowed uneasily. Where could she start? She gazed past Kale and let her eyes wander across the pond toward the bright green fields in the distance and the wide mountain range further out. Her tumultuous emotions felt terribly out of place here where she was surrounded with such beauty. She sighed quietly. She wasn't used to talking about John so openly.

Then she shook her head and went on slowly. "Blaze and I came home from shopping one day. We got home later than usual. I needed some fresh vegetables for dinner, and when I pulled into the driveway, John was standing there, waiting. It was unusual for him to do that, and right away I noticed he looked angry—angrier than normal." She took a deep, shuddering breath.

"When Blaze and I got out of the car, he grabbed Blaze's shoulder. He asked Blaze where we had been, and Blaze seemed really upset. Blaze wasn't usually scared of John, but he had begun to act really differently around his father." She shook her head. "Blaze told him that we had only been to the market, and John pushed Blaze toward the house. He yelled at him to get inside and go upstairs. John never lost his temper anywhere but behind closed doors.

"I asked John what was wrong. I couldn't figure out why he was so upset. Usually he got angry if we came home a little late, but that time I could tell he was enraged. John told me that a friend of his had stopped by earlier to pick up a package that he had left on the entryway table. I remembered then that John had told me about the package before he'd left for work that morning, but I'd forgotten all about it so I wasn't home when his friend came by. I told John I was sorry, but he just got angrier." She tucked her trembling hands tightly in her lap.

Jacey gazed out, unseeing, across the water and went on in an uneven voice. She didn't dare look at Kale as she continued. "John told me to get into the house, so I went in front of him. When we got inside, he slammed the door. He kicked me from behind. I dropped all the groceries and I fell against the stairs. Blaze was standing a few steps up, and he begged John to stop hitting me. I tried to get up. I was afraid John would go after Blaze." She took a deep breath, and her eyes shut, remembering.

"Normally, Blaze never stayed around once John started thrashing me. He had never yelled at his father before either. I tried to get up, but John stomped on my lower back. He slammed my head against the edge of the step. I knew I was bleeding. I thought he had broken my nose. I tried to tell him I was sorry, but he just kept hitting me. I could hear Blaze screaming for him to stop. I tried to get away, but I couldn't." Jacey heard Kale's indrawn breath, and she lowered her head shamefully.

"He grabbed me and slammed my head into the wall. After that, everything went black. The next thing I remember, I woke up in the hospital. I had a severe concussion, and my left arm was broken." She paused when Kale breathed her name, and she swiped at a hot tear sliding down her cheek. She didn't dare look up. She didn't want to see pity in his eyes.

"At first I didn't know what had happened. I panicked

because I didn't know where Blaze was. The nurse told me that Blaze was in the state's custody, and they were keeping him at a special home. John was in jail. Blaze came by later that day and told me that when John didn't stop hitting me, he had run to get Mr. Zulin, our neighbor. Mr. Zulin called the police. Later, when I was able to leave the hospital, I got custody of Blaze. We moved straight to Detroit to live with Melissa. Blaze and I—we've been living with her and her daughter, Jenny, ever since," she finished.

"Jacey," Kale whispered. He slowly reached down for her hands. Then he took her trembling hands in his, and Jacey held her breath. Her heart hammered in her chest as he continued, "I'm sorry, Jacey." He lifted her chin with the tip of his finger.

Refusing to meet his gaze, she pulled away and let her eyes drop to the ground. "I worked with a good lawyer to complete the divorce," she went on. "I was able to do it without any contact with John. I didn't contest anything. I didn't want anything, just custody of Blaze. And with the domestic violence charges, I was able to retain full custody for now. But . . ." She paused, uncertain how to go on. Finally, she allowed her eyes to meet Kale's.

All traces of anger were gone as he encouraged gently, "But what?" He reached for her hand once again. She shivered as his long fingers curled against hers.

Her eyes narrowed nervously, and she cleared her throat. "Last week the FBI tracked me down at the café where I worked in Detroit. They—well, they told me things about John. Things that I never—I had no idea." She stopped and raised a hand to her temple, rubbing it absently.

Kale leaned toward her, and she could smell the familiar scent of his aftershave. "What sort of things did they tell you?" he questioned apprehensively.

Their eyes met, and he nodded encouragingly. "They told me that he and a man named Rafael Vizcaino—well, he and John are involved in money laundering and drugs. The agents said that John might also be involved with the disappearance of a news reporter and a lawyer named Sharon Ivan. John had an affair with her, but they think he may have killed her. They found her body in a warehouse." Jacey stopped when she heard Kale's indrawn breath.

His fingers stiffened against hers, and she looked up to meet his surprised eyes. Her throat felt tight, and she suddenly choked back a sob. "After the FBI told me all this, Melissa and I—we came up with this crazy idea. All this—it sounds so nuts, I know, but I have this feeling that John wants Blaze. If he finds us, I'll never see my son again. And I worry that—" She sniffed loudly. "John has always had power and money, but now, if what the FBI told me is true . . ." She shook her head and went on firmly, "I'm sorry that I came here. Really I am. I didn't know what else to do or where else to go. I panicked. As soon as the FBI told me about John, things seemed to make sense. I believe the things the FBI told me about him. You don't know how scared I am. I hate lying to people, but I'll do anything to protect Blaze. I'm planning on leaving in a few days. Blaze and I are going to Salt Lake. There are several openings for waitresses, and it shouldn't take me long to get a job. I never meant to hurt anyone. I never thought I could love Grant and Helen like I do.

"And Blaze—I've never seen him so attached to anyone like he is to Grant. He's usually so quiet around men." She stopped, then added hurriedly, "But we'll leave now. I never meant to take advantage of anyone. I just wanted to keep Blaze safe."

When Kale dropped her hand, she looked up at him anxiously. He exhaled and rubbed a hand across his face before he eyed Jacey carefully.

"Jacey," he began gruffly, "you can't just disappear. It—it would break Dad's heart if you just left."

"But when he finds out that I'm not Melissa—I'm going to have to tell them," Jacey reminded him.

He nodded knowingly. "They'll understand, Jacey. They might not be too happy about being deceived—no one would—but I know they'll understand."

Jacey shook her head and stared out across the pond. "I'm so confused, Kale. I don't know what to do. I can't hide from John forever. I know that, but—" She sighed wearily.

"What exactly did the FBI agents tell you? Is that all they said?" Kale pressed.

"Yes." She nodded. "They told me exactly what I just told you. They thought that I knew something. I know they didn't believe that I wasn't involved, but I don't know anything about it besides what they told me. I had no idea John was involved in anything like that. John never told me anything that concerned his restaurants or business interests. And after so many years of his verbal and physical abuse, I didn't really care about his business. I simply wrapped myself in a bubble. I focused on keeping John's house going, keeping up appearances, and taking care of Blaze.

"Our marriage was a nightmare. There was always another woman. But I lived for the times when John would show any sign that he cared. He wasn't always a terrible man. Sometimes he would treat me so well, like there was no other woman in the world that mattered. Somehow, I lived for those brief moments. In those instances, I felt certain he could change, but that last time, I knew John would never be the man I dreamed he could be or the man I thought I had married. It took eight years for me to realize that and finally stand up against his threats.

"You have no idea how terrible—how *guilty* I feel for staying so long. The things that Blaze saw John do to me. I cannot begin to imagine what it must be like for a child to watch his father beat his mother into unconsciousness. I really thought—" She shook her head miserably. "I thought that he was going to kill me." Her eyes met Kale's. "I think he would have," she finished, her voice nearly inaudible.

Kale's eyes narrowed. "I'm so sorry, Jacey," he whispered and he gently touched her cheek.

Jacey glanced away anxiously. She had never disclosed so much about her and John's relationship to anyone before, but she didn't want pity.

"Just because you stayed, it doesn't make you a bad mother. You left, which only proves how strong you are. You wanted more for your son, and you did what you had to do to give him a better life. A lot of women stay in that sort of situation all their lives," Kale reminded her. Jacey raised her eyes to meet his. "You're stronger than you realize, Jacey."

"I don't feel strong. I brought my son clear across the country

134

to hide from his father. I've lied and I've taught Blaze that it's all right, as long as we're protecting ourselves. But I didn't know what else to do. I panicked, and when they thought I was involved in all of this, my first thought was to run. If John found us—I don't know what would happen."

"Do you remember the names of the agents?" Kale asked.

She shook her head. "Not really. Agent Ronald and Agent Parks—something like that. At the time, I was in shock, and then to add to it, they treated me like I was withholding information. They made me feel like a criminal. They showed me their badges and told me to contact them if I saw John, but I knew they couldn't protect me from him. If John found us—" She shrugged despondently.

"Listen, Jacey." Kale turned her face gently toward his, and his eyes bore intently into hers. "Stay a little longer—a week at least, all right?" He sighed. "But you're right. You and Blaze can't hide from your ex-husband forever. Once you start working or enroll Blaze in school, you'll be easy to find, and if he's that dangerous, then you'd better stay 'Melissa' until we figure things out. I have a friend in Provo, Paul Ward. He may be able to give you a bit more—" he shrugged. "Well, a bit more help with the situation, but you can't just leave here and expect that John won't find you," he finished.

Jacey sighed heavily and let her gaze drop to the ground. She felt emotionally deflated. "I know that," she whispered. A fat tear rolled down her cheek and across her jawline, then plummeted to the ground. "I've hated lying to your parents, Kale." She looked into his eyes and knew he understood. "I would never want to hurt them. Please believe me. But I don't want their pity either. It's so hard when people know the truth about John and our marriage," she whispered.

He smiled perceptively. "I know, Jacey. I understand—really, I do. I don't like that you came out here and deceived my parents, but I understand why you did it—now." He sighed. "Listen, we'll think of something."

"I'm sure it was quite a shock the first time you saw me." Jacey forced a smile, then added quietly, "Why didn't you say anything?"

Kale shrugged. "I met Blaze first, on the way in from the fields. I knew something was up when Pops introduced me to Melissa's *son*. I knew she had a daughter about that age, then when I saw you—well, like I said, I figured you had to have a pretty good reason for doing what you were doing. I don't know too many people who could come and put on a show as good as you did without a very important reason for doing it. Mom and Pops don't have money, so I knew you wouldn't be after that, and if you *were* after their money—well, then I figured you weren't a very good con artist." He stepped away and moved toward the edge of the pond, then bent to grasp a small rock from its bank and skipped it across the water.

"But why didn't you say anything until now?"

Kale turned to face her, and he shrugged, "I was hoping you would. I thought maybe you would eventually tell one of my parents. I felt so frustrated with you." He laughed humorlessly. "I didn't know who you were or what you were doing here, but every time I tried to talk to you, I couldn't." He shook his head. "I would get so frustrated whenever I'd hear you lie about being Melissa, but the look in your eyes, the way you acted, seemed so contrary to what you were doing. I knew something was wrong. Blaze never spoke about his dad, and you both looked scared to death most of the time."

"I hate lying," she whispered.

"I know you do." He shook his head. "I could see it in your eyes every time, and it left me more confused."

Jacey opened her mouth to reply, then shut it instead. She smiled sadly.

"Nothing about you and Blaze added up, and you certainly didn't look like a couple of criminals. I had planned on forcing the truth out of you last night, but there didn't seem to be a chance, and it left me more frustrated than ever that I had to leave. I was pretty thankful when the office called to tell me my trip was canceled," he finished.

"I'm sorry, Kale," Jacey whispered.

Kale's mouth quirked faintly. "Never mind, Jacey. I understand."

136

Jacey nodded, relieved that he had understood. She could not help but suddenly feel as though a terrible weight had been lifted off her shoulders. She smiled softly.

"I'm glad that you know," Jacey admitted. "And thank you, for listening. You don't know how hard it's been to keep this act up. It isn't me. I've never done anything like this before, but I would do anything to keep John from getting Blaze." She inhaled a breath of fresh air. "And I'm glad to know—well, I thought you either really disliked 'Melissa,' or you just really didn't like me."

Kale chuckled. "Oh, I liked you. In fact, I spent a lot of time trying not to like you. That was the problem. You seemed like a good person, not some con artist, but I just didn't know. That's why I felt so confused. I tried to talk to you a couple of times. I just could never get the words out. I didn't know what to say, and there wasn't a lot of time to talk with Mom and Pops around."

Jacey smiled a little sheepishly, then asked, "When should we tell them? Grant and Helen, I mean."

Kale stepped toward her, and she looked up. Her heart jumped a little as he raised a hand to cup her cheek. His eyes narrowed, and Jacey held her breath expectantly. His hand felt cool against her hot, tear-streaked cheek, and she closed her eyes briefly, relishing the feel of a comforting touch.

"We'll tell them together, in a few days. I want to see what Paul suggests first. Unfortunately, I won't get a chance to talk with him for a few days. As far as I know, he's gone out of town on business." He grinned and shook his head. "Just keep being 'Melissa.' I hate lying too, Jacey, but we're going to need time to talk and think things through. We'll tell Mom and Dad soon, and I feel certain they'll understand. They'll be hurt, but I know they'll do all they can to help. They love you, whether you're Melissa or not."

Jacey's heart felt lighter, and she couldn't help but think she had finally found a friend in Kale.

She smiled into his dark eyes. "Thank you, Kale."

He nodded. Then his touch lingered for a heart-stopping moment, and Jacey could feel his hand tense slightly against her cheek as his eyes dropped toward her trembling mouth. She held her breath, then sighed when his hand dropped to his side and he stepped away. He tore his eyes from hers and shoved his hand into the back pocket of his jeans as he cleared his throat gruffly.

"Don't worry about it, Jacey. Like I said, we'll think of something. Guess we'd better go find Pops and Blaze, huh?"

Jacey turned to stare out toward the water. "We'd better," she agreed, then smiled when a fish jumped, sending a perfect ripple across the smooth surface of the water. "*Now* they're hungry."

She heard Kale laugh. "Once they start jumping, it usually means we're out of luck."

"It's so beautiful here," Jacey commented. Her eyes rose toward the sky as a few ducks flew overhead.

Kale looked up to watch the ducks and nodded his agreement before he turned to face her. "I've got to go into Provo tomorrow. I need to pick up a few supplies for the horses." He shoved his hands into his back pockets before going on. "Ride in with me? We'll have lunch, and it'll give us a chance to talk some more."

Jacey watched him for a second, and a smile touched her lips. "I'd like that," she replied softly.

He nodded, then grinned broadly, and Jacey's heart suddenly flip-flopped. She hadn't seen him smile so openly, and she forced down a sudden blush. He could definitely make a woman's pulse race.

"Well, it's good to finally meet you, Jacey Grayson," he teased, and Jacey laughed freely.

"It's good to meet you too, Kale," she chuckled.

Blaze's voice suddenly reached her ears, and Kale and Jacey turned simultaneously toward the dirt road just as Blaze came into sight.

"Mom! Kale!" the boy yelled. "Come see what I caught! It's a toad!"

Kale laughed loudly and winked at Jacey. She smiled, visibly relived, and waved when Grant came into view, puffing behind Blaze.

"Look, Mom, look!" Blaze panted.

His feet kicked up a thin trail of dust as he skidded down the small slope toward the spot where she and Kale stood. He cupped a round, slimy toad between both hands. His fingers were covered in a greasy-looking mud, and Jacey had to hide her sudden grimace as she examined the slime-coated creature in her son's hand.

"Isn't he neat? I caught him all by myself." Blaze grinned proudly.

Kale laughed as he examined Blaze's toad. "Looks like you caught a big one, kid. Way to go." He ruffled Blaze's hair affectionately.

"The boy's a right good frog hunter," Grant added breathlessly as he joined the group. He laid his and Blaze's poles across the weathered picnic table and grinned at Jacey. "And frogs are about all we caught," he added.

Jacey laughed. "You were lucky. We didn't catch anything." She cocked her head toward her pole, still propped up near the edge of the water. Then she stepped toward her pole, reeled it in quickly, and eyed the dead, pale worm, still hanging from her hook with a grimace.

Kale laughed. "Looks like the only thing we've done is drown a couple of worms," he said good-naturedly.

• • •

Melissa's arms tightened convulsively as the stranger turned a sharp corner too fast, then she swore as he negotiated her Ford Focus through the crowded streets of Detroit's suburbs. Jenny whimpered quietly and wiggled against Melissa's tight embrace. Melissa glanced down at her trembling daughter and loosened her crushing grip.

"Where is he taking us?" Jenny's heated breath brushed across Melissa's neck.

Melissa shuddered. "I—I don't know."

What am I going to do? Where is he taking us? Melissa buried her face against Jenny's hair and tried to still her trembling body. She felt weak with panic.

After John Trent had disappeared, the stranger had immediately forced Melissa and Jenny into the car at gun point. He hadn't said more than two words, and his silence terrified Melissa. She had asked him several questions without a single answer in return.

"Where are you taking us?" she tried again.

The man stared ahead without any indication that he had heard.

"Where are you taking us!" she yelled, panic tainting her voice. Melissa forced another onslaught of tears back as the man, again, made no indication that he had heard her question.

Jenny whimpered quietly, and Melissa whispered against her brow, "It's all right. It's going to be all right, toots."

A moment later, the stranger made another sharp turn. Melissa gasped as the car shot quickly around a bend and entered a shadowed, narrow alleyway. The car slowed, then came to an abrupt stop. The blood in Melissa's veins ran cold as the man glanced back toward them. He stepped from the car and jerked open the back door. Jenny squeaked. Melissa's arms constricted around her daughter's trembling body. She scooted further against the opposite door.

"Get out of the car." The man bent and eyed Melissa closely.

She shook her head, terrified.

"Get out," he repeated slowly.

Melissa stiffened, and the man grunted before he deftly reached in to grasp Jenny's leg. Jenny's shrill scream rent the tense silence. Melissa jerked instinctively. Turning her body, she kicked at his face. The man cursed as his grip slipped on Jenny's leg, and he reached for his gun. Melissa froze at the sight of the revolver swinging toward her daughter.

"I said to get out. Now!" he spoke gruffly.

Jenny peered fearfully toward the man, and Melissa could feel the little girl's hot tears running onto her forearms. Pushing Jenny's rigid body behind her, Melissa used her own body to shield her daughter as she stepped from the car. The man stepped back, allowing her room, and Melissa stood, her body tense.

The corners of the man's mouth quirked faintly as he held the gun casually toward Melissa. "Get your girl out of the car," he told her quietly.

"What are you going to do to us?" Melissa whispered.

He inhaled and his nostrils flared, then he shook his head. "Woman, you'd better do what I tell you, if you want to live," he answered almost inaudibly.

Melissa's eyes narrowed, and she studied his expression carefully. *Live?* she questioned silently. She was beginning to feel hysterical.

"Who are you? What are you going to do to us?" she whispered hoarsely.

The man shook his head before he replied quietly, "Just do as I say."

Melissa's heart pounded uncertainly. Then, with a quaking breath, she turned toward the door and reached in, pulling Jenny gently from the car.

Melissa whispered, "Stay behind me." Jenny nodded, and Melissa turned to face the man with wide, questioning eyes.

He nodded and stepped away, lowering his gun. He fixed his gaze firmly on Melissa and Jenny as he stepped around to the back of her car and opened the trunk. Melissa's eyes widened, and she gasped, gripping Jenny's arm tightly.

"Get in the trunk." He stepped back toward them and raised his gun when Melissa stiffened. She shoved Jenny back against the car.

The man smiled derisively. "Uh-uh." He moved quickly to shut the car door, and Melissa jumped when his hand suddenly grasped her arm.

His long, lean fingers dug into her fleshy, upper arm and she grimaced. "No," she whispered, pleading.

His eyes bore into hers. He jerked her forward, and she stumbled slightly. Melissa could smell his expensive aftershave, and she grimaced when his breath brushed across her flushed cheek.

"Lady," he whispered, "we don't have a lot of time. Get in the trunk."

Melissa's eyes narrowed skeptically, and he nodded ever so slightly. She tried to read the unspoken message in his dark eyes, but the thought of willingly stepping into the car's trunk was too much to endure. What did he want? Filled with uncertainty, she shook her head, eyeing the trunk with a horror-filled expression. Was he going to leave them there? Would they ever get out?

"I—" she began and the man suddenly gave her a little shake.

His eyes narrowed with frustration, and he pulled her toward the gaping trunk. Jenny clung to Melissa's free arm, and Melissa struggled against her captor's painful grip. She struck out with her foot, kicking the man hard in his shin. He groaned angrily. Abruptly, he let Melissa go and pulled his gun up toward her face.

"You are making this a lot harder than it has to be, woman. Get in the trunk. Now!"

"No!" Melissa's heart pounded deafeningly in her ears, and the man cursed before he suddenly lunged for her.

His thick arms encircled Melissa's slim waist, and she struggled desperately against his crushing grasp. Jenny's scream echoed against the narrow alley walls as he tossed Melissa easily into the trunk. *No!* her mind screamed. She struggled to get out just as the man reached for Jenny. Jenny fought wildly against his grip, and he cursed loudly when Jenny's teeth sunk into his arm.

"Shut up," he said, tossing Jenny's small body in against Melissa.

They both cried loudly as the trunk's lid bore down on them and closed with a deafening thump. Darkness engulfed them. Melissa choked on her fear. Jenny sobbed uncontrollably, and Melissa shifted in the tight space. She wrapped her arms around her daughter's quivering body. She felt as if she would suffocate. She pushed hard against the trunk's lid with her hip. Jenny screamed, and Melissa pressed her face against Jenny's.

"It's okay, shhh. It's all right," Melissa whispered into the inky blackness.

She gasped loudly when she felt the car start, and her stomach turned sickeningly as the car lurched forward.

"It's okay," she repeated. She kissed her daughter's damp brow. Jenny continued to sob, and Melissa's tears joined hers.

THIRTEEN

Afternoon quickly faded into dusk, and Jacey, Blaze, Kale, and Grant spent the rest of the daylight hours exploring the ponds. Each little pond held new discoveries. Kale took Jacey and Blaze around the fishing pond to find the heron's nest on the opposite bank, and they were amazed at the other little fowl nests tucked here and there among the tall reeds.

Blaze found a rope tied to a tree limb, and Kale showed him how to swing out over the water and land back on the bank. They all laughed, watching Kale's strong, tall body swing from the rope, and Jacey held her breath when Blaze took his first turn. His face lit with exhilaration as his body swung across the water, and he laughed excitedly when Kale caught him.

As dusk faded into night, Kale and Grant built a small fire in a cement ring next to one of the larger ponds. They feasted on roasted hot dogs and marshmallows. Blaze was amazed that they could actually cook a hot dog over an open fire, and he laughed with delight when his first hot dog came out burnt and withered.

"Now you have to eat it," Jacey teased as Blaze grimaced.

"Uh-uh. I cooked this one for you, Mom," he gibed back.

Jacey laughed and turned her hot dog over the bright flames. The smell made her stomach growl hungrily. All around them, the night was filled with unfamiliar sounds and scuttles, yet Jacey felt content and unafraid as she sat next to Kale. She glanced his way, smiling timidly when she caught his eye. He grinned, and the butterflies kicked up in her stomach. She had truly enjoyed getting to know the lighter side of Kale.

Jacey knew that Kale had had a difficult time referring to her as Melissa throughout the rest of the day, and it made her realize that she would soon have to talk with Grant and Helen. The thought turned her stomach, but Kale felt certain they would understand. On that thought, her heart took courage. The knowledge that she could finally be rid of this deception left her feeling somewhat relieved. However, she still felt an underlying sense of panic. Kale had assured her that he would stand by her when she explained herself. She silently wondered how Grant would take the news that she was not, after all, his long-lost niece. The thought of Grant's pain left Jacey terribly anxious.

"Mom, your hot dog's burning," Blaze called, and Jacey laughed, pulling her hot dog from the fire.

She grinned sheepishly, then laughed when Blaze popped a gooey marshmallow in his mouth. "You'd better save some of those for me." Jacey gave a sudden startled gasp when a loud splash sounded in the water near them.

She turned toward Kale. The bright flames cast shadows across his face, and he grinned playfully. "Beaver."

Her eyes widened in surprise. "Really?"

Blaze moved next to Kale and peered into the dark pond.

Kale laughed. "There he is. Can you see him?" He pointed out a faint ripple in the water. "He's swimming across, there."

"Whoa," Blaze breathed. "I can see him—can you, Mom?"

Jacey shook her head and moved closer to Kale. She peered into the darkness and shook her head.

"I can't," she spoke quietly.

Kale placed his arm around her shoulder. Jacey caught her bottom lip between her teeth when his face moved near hers. She could feel his warm breath brush across her cheek.

"He's there," Kale pointed with his free arm.

Jacey grinned when she saw the little trail of ripples across the water. "Oh, I see him," she whispered. Kale's eyes met hers, and he smiled lightly before he moved away.

"Boy, I'm stuffed," Blaze commented when he and Jacey moved back toward the fire. The flames leapt high, and shadows danced across on his young face as he yawned.

Grant laughed softly. "Probably should be heading back now. Besides, these skeeters think I'm a dang blood donor," he muttered.

They all laughed.

• • •

"That boy's clear worn out," Grant said as he pulled into the darkened driveway.

Jacey smiled and glanced at her sleeping son. His dark head rested against Kale's broad shoulder, his breathing even and deep.

"I'll carry him upstairs for you," Kale whispered, and their eyes met just as the porch light flipped on, casting a faint glow across the yard.

"Thanks," she returned, stepping from the truck.

She turned to watch Kale scoot across the truck's seat, being careful not to bump Blaze. He stepped from the truck and lifted the sleeping boy easily in his arms. Then he glanced toward Jacey once more before he turned toward the house, carrying Blaze inside and up the stairs to his room. He laid Blaze down, and Jacey stepped around to the other side of the bed in order to remove Blaze's shoes and pants before she tucked him under the quilt. Blaze stirred, sighed, and fell back asleep. She leaned over to kiss his forehead.

"Thank you for carrying him up. He wore himself out today." She touched her son's hair gently before she looked at Kale. He was watching Blaze closely. Emotion stirred in his eyes, and Jacey couldn't help but wonder at the sadness she read in his expression.

His eyes rose toward hers. He smiled wanly and then cleared his throat. "I haven't been in this room in a long while," he commented as he walked toward the dresser to pick up a small stone. He rolled the rock across his fingers before he placed it back in the box.

"Blaze loves this room," Jacey replied. "Uncle Grant said that you made the bed and side tables."

He nodded. "Long time ago. I found those stumps up in the hills, back where I built my house."

"They're beautiful. I've never seen anything quite like them."

He rubbed his hand across the stump's smooth top. "Well, it was a while ago."

He smiled faintly and stepped toward the door just as Jacey whispered his name. He paused and turned to face her. Light from the hallway cast shadows across the strong angles of his face, and Jacey caught her breath apprehensively.

"What is it?" he asked, his tone low.

"I just wanted . . . to thank you for today. For understanding—and for being so willing to help."

Kale nodded as he glanced at Blaze then back toward Jacey. "You're welcome—Jacey," he spoke her name quietly.

Jacey nodded, and watched him carefully. "I think I'll go get washed up before I come back downstairs. Are you—are you staying?" she asked, hoping that she didn't sound too expectant.

A smile touched Kale's lips. "I think I'll head back in to my place now. I really should check on Red and Avatar." He grinned, and Jacey chuckled.

"That really meant a lot to him, you know—letting him name the foal and giving him the arrowhead."

Kale nodded and smiled. "He's a great kid, Jacey."

"Well—thank you again."

"I'll see you tomorrow." He stepped into the hall and then turned. "Still want to ride into town with me?"

Jacey nodded. "Yes."

His smile broadened. "Great. I'll see you tomorrow—Melissa." He grinned, and Jacey smiled sheepishly. Then he added, "Try to not worry. I'm beginning to think we should probably tell them tomorrow, though. I'm not so good at this. I nearly blew it tonight—and more than once. You never did look like a Melissa."

"I want to tell them. You have no idea how guilty I've felt," Jacey admitted.

Kale winked. "I enjoyed today. I'll see you tomorrow."

He waved and turned down the hall. Jacey could hear his heavy footfalls descend the stairs. She sighed and stepped across the hall to her room. She could hear Kale's deep baritone voice talking with Grant downstairs, and she raised a hand to her tense stomach.

She truly did hope that Grant and Helen would understand. Jacey knew that no excuse was worth the lies she had told. She shook her head and stole a glance at her weary expression in the mirror. The day had definitely brought optimism, but she felt emotionally fatigued. She sighed, deciding a hot shower would work wonders on her exhausted state.

She gathered her pajamas and turned to leave the room just as she caught sight of her cell phone sitting atop the dresser. She picked it up to check the calls. Melissa had not yet called back, and Jacey grimaced. She had forgotten all about Melissa's call that afternoon. She punched in Melissa's number and listened while it rang four times before connecting once again to her voice mail.

Jacey sighed. *They're probably out to the movies*, she thought. Melissa usually took Jenny out a couple of times a week, and they were always out quite late. She put the phone back inside the top dresser drawer. *I'll try again in the morning*, she told herself as she stepped out into the hall.

"I'm not going on a diet, woman. You bake cookies and then expect me to eat horse food?" Grant's teasing tone echoed from down in the dining room. Jacey paused in the hall and smiled. She could smell freshly baked cookies, and Helen's soft laughter floated up the stairs.

Jacey smiled as Helen returned, "You think that's horse food? You just consider yourself lucky I don't send you out to eat in the barn with them horses."

She heard Grant's deep grumbling laughter, and Jacey smiled as she stepped into the bathroom. She would shower, then sneak downstairs for a couple of cookies.

• • •

Melissa took another deep breath, and her arms tightened around her sleeping daughter. The darkness seemed to press in around her, and she fought the urge to scream. She pushed against the side of the car, trying to relieve the numbness in her legs from staying in such a cramped position. Nausea stirred in the depths of her stomach when she felt the vehicle turn sharply around another corner. She closed her eyes. Where was he taking them? What was going to happen to her and Jenny? She had lost track of how long they had been in the suffocating darkness.

She felt panic press against her chest once again and she gulped another lungful of stale air. Jenny stirred slightly, and Melissa pressed her face against her daughter's hair. She readjusted her arm to better cushion Jenny's head.

Suddenly she felt the car come to a stop and she heard the gears shift as the car jerked into park. Melissa's heart pounded maddeningly, and she waited with bated breath. Where were they? What was happening?

Jenny stirred again, and Melissa whispered urgently, "Shhh."

"Mom," Jenny's weak voice spoke against her arm.

"Shhh, we've stopped," she uttered against Jenny's brow.

She felt her young daughter tense, and Melissa instinctively pushed against the lid of the trunk with the small of her back. Suddenly she heard the unmistakable sound of the key in the lock, and the trunk lid flew open. Blinding light pushed the darkness away, and Melissa shut her eyes against the sudden brightness.

"No," she yelled when their attacker reached down. She felt his strong fingers grasp her arm. She jerked away, and Jenny sobbed loudly.

"Calm down, Ms. McCoy. You're safe now. No one's going to hurt you," a strangely familiar voice called from somewhere behind the man. Melissa froze. Glancing up warily, she strained to see against the brightness.

"Come on out. Let me help you," the man who had taken them captive spoke directly above her, and Melissa peered up at him, stunned.

"What—what's going on?" she asked as he grabbed her arm again.

This time she allowed him to pull her out. She stepped out of the tight trunk. Her legs wobbled unsteadily as blood rushed back, achingly, to her numb limbs. She caught sight of Agent Ronald, and her eyes broadened.

"Mom?" Melissa heard Jenny's strained voice, and she turned to help her daughter from the trunk.

"Ms. McCoy," Agent Ronald stepped closer, and Melissa turned in his direction.

"What's going on? Where are we? What are you doing?" Melissa glanced around the empty garage. The walls were made of steel, and the sagging wooden roof looked as if it would crash down on them at any moment. The place smelt strongly of gas fumes. She realized it was dark outside, and a bright halogen lantern lit the area inside the garage.

Her eyes narrowed as she glanced between the men. "What's going on?" she said, suppressing a sob.

"Ms. McCoy, there is no need to worry. Sal here is Special Agent Nick Salvatore. He's with the FBI. Sal's one of our undercover agents—"

Melissa shook her head, grasping the edge of the trunk for support, "You're—you're FBI?" she questioned skeptically. Sal nodded, and Melissa's eyes shot toward Agent Ronald. "He doesn't work for John?"

Agent Ronald shook his head, and she heard Sal laugh quietly. "No, Ms. McCoy. I don't work for John Trent—at least, not technically. I've brought you and your daughter to an undisclosed location—"

Agent Ronald jumped in, "You're safe, Ms. McCoy. Agent Salvatore had to make things look genuine. We're sorry to have had to frighten you, but—"

"I had to do my job. I had to get you and your daughter out of the city, undetected," Sal cut in.

"And we had no other choice," Agent Ronald continued. "Agent Salvatore contacted Agent Parker and me as soon as he knew he could get you and your daughter to safety. I'm afraid to say we were unaware of the situation beforehand. Agent Salvatore arranged for me to meet you here."

Melissa's eyes narrowed. "I can't believe this," she whispered in shock. "I—Jacey, is she all right? You arrested John?"

The agents glanced at one another before Agent Ronald answered. "No," he replied slowly. "We haven't arrested John

Trent yet, Ms. McCoy. There are certain—"

Melissa's eyes narrowed. "What do you mean? I don't understand this. What about Jacey? What about us? You—I thought—you made me believe you were going to kill us. John tried to have us killed. What is going on?" Her voice grew increasingly louder.

"Calm down, Ms. McCoy. Let me try to explain." Agent Ronald stepped closer, and Melissa instinctively took a step back. "You are safe, I can assure you. John Trent hired Agent Salvatore to find Jacey Grayson. He tracked Grayson to you and reported back to John Trent. Yes, we understand that his intentions were to have you and your daughter harmed, but you need to understand that we have been investigating John Trent and the Vizcaino crime gang for months. We think John Trent's intention is to find his son. But we're not certain what his objective is with regard to his ex-wife. Also, John Trent is highly involved with the Vizcaino organization, and we need to consider our investigation."

"What do you mean?" Melissa exploded. "John Trent tried to have me and my daughter killed, by this guy here," she jerked a finger toward Sal, "and you're telling me you can't arrest him? Isn't this enough? If he finds Jacey—don't you get it? He'll kill her! And you—you scared us half to death."

Sal held up his hands. "Calm down. Listen, I understand, but you need to understand that we can't arrest Trent until we have enough solid evidence against him to put him away for a long time."

"He wanted you to kill us! I—do you know what you've put us through?" Melissa yelled, glaring at the two men.

Jenny stirred behind Melissa, and she gave her daughter's hand a quick squeeze. "It's all right, toots."

Agent Ronald shook his head. "I'm sorry to say that we need to consider our investigation. Charges will be brought against John for what he has done to you, but we need to wait and see if he approaches Jacey Grayson and what his purposes are. If he approaches her in a way that we feel is at all forceful, we will be able to make an arrest and book him on double charges. But you need to realize that a man like John Trent has friends in high places. With this charge alone, he would be out on bail within the week, and your friend would still be in danger. Try to understand. We've been attempting to bring down the Vizcaino crime organization for several months now. We will do what we can to protect your friend, but we need more to put John Trent away for good."

"Ms. McCoy," Sal jumped in, "John Trent belongs to a fairly strong crime ring. He has rank and position within this organization, but John Trent's obsession with his ex-wife just may be the key to this outfit's undoing. If we're able to bring more charges against him, we have more of a chance that he'll agree to a plea bargain. We need his cooperation and any information he can give us on the Vizcaino family to back up my investigation. But unless he attempts to harm Jacey Grayson, we really don't have a lot to hold him. I understand he tried to have you 'taken care of,' but we need more, and there's nothing that says a man can't see his ex-wife and kid. Besides, if we were to arrest John Trent now, my cover would be blown. And right now, I'm in a critical position. I took a huge risk tonight," Sal finished.

Melissa's legs felt weak, and she took a deep calming breath. "So you'll wait until he kills her? If he finds her, you know he'll kill her," Melissa defended.

"We will do the best we can," Agent Ronald replied. "We can really only *assume* that his intention is to harm Jacey Trent—"

"His intentions *are* to harm her," Melissa cut in bitingly. "You—you told me that John had issued a contract on Jacey. He wants her dead," she finished angrily.

Sal exhaled noisily, running a hand through his short, black hair. "The contract he issued was through me. I work mostly out of Chicago, but I happened to be in town. The Vizcaino organization runs a few jobs out of Detroit. John knew I was in Detroit, and he knew his ex-wife was here, so he came to find me. He paid me a grand to *find* her, not *kill* her. I contacted the Special Agent in Charge in the Chicago field office. My SAC contacted Agent Ronald and Agent Parker here in Detroit. They want any information Jacey Grayson can give them on John Trent. So, we don't really know Trent's intentions, and as I said before, the Bureau will do what it can to protect her and her son. If he does attempt to harm either of them, we will have enough to book him for a longer period and hopefully reach a plea bargain."

"Ms. McCoy," Agent Ronald spoke, "Agent Parker is on his way now to contact the field office in Utah. Sal told us about John Trent's plan. We can get a squad car to keep an eye on your relatives' place. We'll post Trent and Rafael Vizcaino's descriptions with the local police departments and put them on high alert. They'll watch closely. If it looks as if he's going to pose any sort of threat to Grayson or her son, they'll apprehend him immediately."

"As for you and your daughter, until Trent is secured, you'll need to stay in our custody," Sal added. "Agent Ronald will transport you to the Detroit Field Office, and from there the Special Agent in Charge will give you more details. I'm going to dump your car in the river, staging your deaths in order to protect my cover. We'll report it found in a few days. The FBI will then report your deaths as accidental—which is exactly what Trent had in mind."

Melissa shook her head, overwhelmed, and Sal smiled reassuringly. "Don't worry, Ms. McCoy." He turned toward Agent Ronald. "Well, I'm heading out. I'll do this thing, then see what I can find out."

He turned his attention back toward Melissa. "Sorry to give you such a bad scare. Didn't mean to rough you up so much, but it was the only way to get you safely here. The Vizcaino family may not be especially large, but they have a lot of eyes."

He winked at Jenny, and she shrank against Melissa's side.

"Good luck." He nodded before he moved back to the car and slid into the driver's seat.

The closing door echoed in the large empty garage, and Melissa winced.

"I'll escort you and your daughter to the field office now. You'll receive more information there." Agent Ronald stepped closer and grasped Melissa's elbow gently. "I have a car parked out on the other side of the building," he told her reassuringly.

Melissa nodded numbly and grasped Jenny's hand tightly in her own.

• • •

Jacey stepped toward the mirror to give herself one last decisive glance before she applied a thin coat of lipstick.

"I'm sorry, Blaze, but you just can't go this time," she repeated as she caught sight of Blaze's moping face in the reflection. She turned and smiled knowingly.

"Why can't I go? It's not fair, Mom," he said grumpily.

She shook her head and moved toward the bed to sit next to him. "Not this time," she replied firmly. She bent to pull on her worn tennis shoes. "You stay here and help Uncle Grant with your horse."

"I already fed Ocotillo, and Aunt Helen already got all the eggs, and Uncle Grant's eating." He scowled.

Jacey laughed and placed her arm around Blaze's shoulders, "I'm sure you'll find plenty to entertain yourself with today, babe."

His head hung dejectedly, and he shrugged out of Jacey's embrace, then stood and sulked back toward his room. Jacey sighed and shook her head, exasperated. She knew that Blaze didn't understand why he couldn't come with her and Kale, but she wasn't ready to let him know that Kale knew their secret. Until she talked with Grant and Helen, Blaze couldn't know.

She stood and glanced out the window. She could see Kale's large Dodge moving up the lane toward the house. A thick trail of dust kicked up behind his truck and floated lazily along the narrow road. She brought a hand to her edgy stomach and swallowed hard, feeling nervous for today. Then moving toward the mirror one last time, she suddenly wondered if she should have worn her hair up, instead of down. *Why is it suddenly so important to look good for Kale?* she asked herself. Up until yesterday, he had only left her feeling disconcerted and angry.

"I don't know what's wrong with me," she muttered to the ceramic chicken staring back at her. "I despised him just a day ago."

She shook her head, frustrated with herself, just as her eye fell on her cell phone sitting on the dresser. She grasped the small phone and placed it inside her purse before she stepped across the hall toward Blaze's room. The door was shut, and she knocked.

When he didn't answer, she opened it and said, "Blaze, Kale's coming. I need to go, babe."

Blaze's back faced her as he sat in front of the television, watching cartoons. His shrug was the only sign that he had heard her.

"Blaze," Jacey sighed.

"Okay, bye," he muttered angrily.

"Please be good. Mind Uncle Grant and Aunt Helen, all right?" she implored before she closed the door. She groaned and exhaled loudly before she descended the stairs.

"Good morning, Uncle Grant." She forced a smile when she stepped down into the dining room.

He whistled playfully. "Good morning, sweetheart." He stood to hug Jacey and kissed her soundly on her cheek. "Boy, it's not every day I get to kiss two beautiful women."

Jacey blushed and laughed.

"Are you hungry, dear? Kale just pulled in, but I'm sure he wouldn't mind if you ate a bit of breakfast before you two take off." Helen came around to give Jacey a quick hug.

She shook her head. "I'm really not very hungry, but thank you anyway."

"Well, if you're sure." Helen patted Jacey's hand.

Jacey followed Helen into the kitchen to pour herself a glass of milk. She paused when she heard the loud bang of the screen door and watched with bated breath as Kale stepped into the house. He caught sight of Jacey and greeted her with a broad smile before he moved to give Helen a quick hug.

"Morning, Mother," he spoke to Helen before he turned his attention back to Jacey. "Morning . . . Melissa."

"Good morning, Kale," she returned as Kale stepped toward the table where Uncle Grant sat finishing his breakfast.

"Morning, Pops. I got the list of feed we need, and I'm picking up a few tack supplies. Do you need anything else while we're out?" Kale picked up a piece of toast and quickly spread a generous slab of butter across its crisp surface. Jacey took a moment to swallow down her milk while Kale ate his toast.

"I think that list about does it. I can't think of much else, son," Grant replied.

"I'll have my cell phone if you think of anything," he informed Grant before he turned to Jacey with a questioning glance. "Where's Blaze?"

She shook her head and gave him a dry smile. "Upstairs, sulking."

Kale chuckled, and Helen added, "We'll find something to keep his mind off his troubles. You two just go on and have a good time."

"Are you ready?" Kale asked, grabbing another slice of toast.

"I am." Jacey nodded before she turned to Helen. "Thank you for keeping an eye on Blaze for me."

"You know we'd watch that boy day or night. He's a joy to have around," Helen replied with a broad smile. "Go on. Have fun and enjoy an afternoon off. Heaven knows a day away from her children is few and far between for a mother."

FOURTEEN

Jacey bit down on her bottom lip uncertainly as Kale exited the freeway in Provo. He had been quiet during the drive, and Jacey wondered if he had changed his mind about helping her. She was working up the nerve to broach the question when his voice suddenly broke through the silence.

"That phone call yesterday morning—was that Melissa?"

Startled, Jacey nodded. "Yes it was. I—"

"What did she want?" Kale cut in.

"I don't know. I've called her a few times, but I haven't been able to get in touch with her. Melissa usually doesn't keep her cell phone with her. She keeps it in the car while she's at work, and she's terrible at returning calls," Jacey admitted.

"You seemed shocked that she called. Has she called before?"

Jacey shook her head again. "No, and it concerns me that she did call. We agreed not to contact each other until I was living in Salt Lake, but it's possible she just wanted to make sure that we made it out here safely. I suppose there could have been a number of reasons she tried to call. I wish I could get a hold of her, though. It's making me uneasy that I can't reach her."

"Has John ever met her?" Kale fired another question, and Jacey looked at him curiously.

"He's met her only a couple of times," she admitted. "I don't know if he would remember her or not. I tried not to mention my friendship with Melissa to him. I knew if he thought we were very close, he would want to cut me off from her."

Kale nodded but remained silent as he navigated his truck through the traffic. Soon he pulled into the crowded parking lot of the local feed store. Jacey glanced around curiously. Several trucks similar to Kale's were parked in the lot. Three men were loading feed bags into the back of another truck, parked closer to the front of the small brick building, and two older men laughed and joked with one another as a young store employee groaned under the weight of the large sack.

The boy dropped the sack into the back of the truck, kicking up a cloud of dust into the air. The two older men slapped the kid on the back, and Jacey could hear their strident laughter when Kale opened his door and stepped out. He shut the door and walked around to assist Jacey from the truck. When their eyes met, he smiled suddenly.

"Hey, I didn't mean to make you worry. I'm sorry, Jacey. I was just curious," he reassured her as he extended his hand.

She stepped from the truck, and Kale laughed, waving his hand toward the store. "Welcome to the feed store." Jacey couldn't help but smile. "I only have a few things to pick up. It won't take too long. Afterward, I thought maybe you'd like to take a ride up the canyon toward Bridal Veil Falls before lunch. I think you'd enjoy seeing it. Would that be all right?"

"I'd like that," Jacey agreed as she followed Kale into the little building.

The tinkling of a bell announced their presence, and Jacey let her eyes adjust to the difference in light as they stepped into a crowded aisle. Immediately, Jacey was encircled by the unmistakable smell of leather and a musty odor she couldn't quite define. She wrinkled her nose. The odd smell was overwhelming. She heard Kale chuckle.

"That's the silage you're smelling. It's fermenting hay and alfalfa. Farmers bale the grass while it's still wet, and then wrap it tightly in plastic. It ferments for a while, and then it's great to feed livestock. Local farmers sell it here during this time of year." Kale informed her with a knowing grin.

He quickly purchased several bags of feed for his animals and Jacey watched, interested, as he and another store employee loaded the large sacks into the back of Kale's Dodge. She couldn't help but enjoy watching Kale work. He lifted the large sack effortlessly, and Jacey tried to ignore the muscles that bunched under his tight T-shirt. Once the last sack was loaded, he stepped toward the truck box to pull a plastic tarp from inside. His eyes caught Jacey's, and he nodded toward the mountains.

"Looks like we might be seeing the falls in the rain." He pointed up toward the rolling, black clouds that had suddenly appeared above the tall peaks.

Amazed, Jacey eyed the approaching storm. The skies had been clear only half an hour before. "That was fast," she commented.

Kale deftly secured the tarps across the bags of feed before he jumped down from the truck's bed and came to stand next her. "Storms in Utah tend to move in fast and hard, but they don't last long. You ready to head out?" he asked, smiling broadly.

Jacey allowed Kale to help her into the truck, and they headed east toward the high mountains that stood above the city. Jacey was amazed at how high the peaks stood above the valley.

"They're so—majestic," she commented as they drew nearer. She gazed with wonder at the high peaks and the rolling, black clouds that surrounded the mountain.

"One day, when we get more time, I'd like to take you to see Mount Timpanogos. I know Blaze would love it. You can see a great view of its summit from this side of the canyon."

She watched with wide eyes as their vehicle dipped under an overpass, and they drove directly next to sheer granite walls. Moments later the narrow canyon entrance opened wide, and Jacey was astonished at the majestic beauty.

"The city built a recreation trail back there along the river. The trail starts out by Utah Lake, goes up past BYU, and then up to Vivian Park. Bridal Veil Falls is along that trail. There are a couple of smaller falls further up past the main falls, but you can usually just catch glimpses of them from the highway," Kale explained as they traveled toward towering rock-layered peaks in the distance.

"Wow," Jacey exclaimed as they neared the mountain. "I've never seen anything like that." She indicated the various layers.

Kale chuckled quietly. "That's Cascade Mountain, and those strange layers are referred to as folded limestone. The waves were created through a process called diagenesis. Basically lots of pressure was applied while the rock was still pliable—soft. The geology of this canyon is pretty amazing," he finished.

Jacey grinned. He sounded like a geologist. "Well, it's beautiful." He caught her eye and winked.

Only a few miles into the canyon, Kale pulled off the highway and into a wide parking area surrounded with oak and giant pines. A few cars were parked in the lot, and as Kale shifted the truck into park, he glanced at Jacey with a cautious smile then spoke, "Looks like we aren't going to have a lot of time before this storm dumps on us. You still feel up to trying to see the falls?"

Jacey laughed and eyed the thick clouds overhead. "I don't melt when I get wet."

Kale smiled broadly and jumped from the driver's seat. After grabbing a denim jacket from the backseat, he came around to her side. Grasping her hand tightly in his, he helped her from the truck and pulled her gently toward the path. "It's not too far up," he informed her, giving her hand a quick squeeze.

Jacey gazed around in wonder at the beautiful park and the wooded area as they traversed the paved trail. The air felt thick with the promise of the impending storm, and she breathed in the moist, fragrant air.

"That's the Provo River," Kale yelled above the din of rushing water. "There are some great fishing spots along this river, especially fly fishing."

"This is gorgeous," Jacey called back.

Suddenly a loud clap of thunder sounded overhead. The crack echoed off the steep canyon walls, and Jacey flinched. Kale smiled and squeezed her hand reassuringly.

As they neared the falls, the sound of rushing water intensified to a nearly roaring pitch. Mist rose in smokelike tendrils, and Jacey caught sight of an amazingly clear pool as they rounded the last bend before reaching the falls. The falls rose high against the mountainside, the top disappearing in the low-hanging clouds.

"This is a double cataract fall. It rises a little over six hundred feet," Kale explained above the noise.

"This is amazing," Jacey replied.

Kale went on. "A few years ago an avalanche destroyed this area. This used to be a pretty popular tourist development." Kale turned to point at the dilapidated, graffiti-covered remains of a building, just across the path. "That used to be the gift store. They ran a tram up to the top, where they built a restaurant. It had an amazing view."

Kale pointed toward a building sitting on the edge of a high precipice. Jacey's mouth fell open.

"That?" she pointed up toward the building. "That would scare me to death. It looks like it would topple right over the edge."

Kale laughed. "It wasn't as bad as it looks from down here."

"What a shame they didn't rebuild," Jacey commented, turning back toward the broken building across the path. She could see the rusted pulley's wheel sticking from the wreckage.

"This area is too unsteady. They deal with snow avalanches up here nearly every winter. When the weather's good, you can hike a fair ways up the falls. This place is usually packed with people. Guess we came on a good day."

He smiled just as thunder clapped overhead. Lightning sliced through the black clouds, and Jacey eyed the storm warily. Another boom overhead sent a few rain drops crashing to the ground, and Jacey shivered instinctively as several fat drops landed on her shoulder.

"I think that's our cue to leave." Kale laughed, placing his jacket across Jacey's shoulders.

Jacey murmured her thanks as she shrugged into the stiff coat. It smelt like horses and Kale's aftershave, and she couldn't hold back a smile. Another loud clap sounded overhead, and then the rain began in earnest. Kale chuckled, pulled his hat from his head, and dropped it onto Jacey's head. She grinned as it fell down across her ears and eyes. Pulling the brim up, she caught his gaze. He winked and took her hand firmly in his.

"Let's make a run for it," he called above the noise of the storm.

Jacey laughed lightheartedly as they jogged down the trail. She stumbled slightly when two bikers zipped past and chuckled sheepishly. Kale grinned as he reached for her waist, and they continued on toward the truck. Once at the truck, Kale rushed to open the passenger door, and Jacey stepped into the high truck and out of the rain. She laughed when water ran down along the brim of Kale's hat and dripped onto her lap. She took it from her head and handed it back to Kale.

She met his amused eyes as he accepted his hat. He gave it a quick shake, and then placed it back onto his wet head. Water dripped from the ends of his hair and fell onto his broad shoulders.

"You're soaked," Jacey commented with a quick laugh. "Thanks for the hat."

"Looked better on you than it does on me." He grinned.

His eyes ran across the contours of her face before his gaze came to rest on her smiling mouth. Suddenly his expression sobered, and Jacey held her breath expectantly. He paused. She watched him anxiously as his eyes rose to meet hers briefly. The corners of his mouth pulled up in a crooked smile before he shut her door and moved around to settle into the driver's seat.

As they made the short drive back toward the city, Kale pointed out various spots of interest. When they passed Brigham Young University, Jacey asked, "Did you go to school here?"

Kale nodded. "They have an excellent earth science program."

Jacey watched with interest as they drove around the campus. Young students carrying heavy book bags walked down the sidewalks, and Jacey was amazed at the appearance of the many students she saw.

"Is this school strictly for Mormons?" she asked, interested.

"No," he replied, "you don't necessarily have to be a member to attend. But all the students have to adhere to the moral virtues of the Church. The curriculum also includes religious classes. There are classes that teach our Church's history and beliefs and other courses on the Book of Mormon and the Bible."

Jacey nodded thoughtfully. "Helen says your sister, Allison, attends here."

Kale pointed. "Ally lives just up there, back behind the stadium. You'll get a chance to meet her this weekend."

"Helen says she's getting married."

Kale smiled wryly. "Yeah—kid named Tom Ernie."

The odd note in his voice caused Jacey to eye him skeptically. She watched him for a moment before she asked, "Is he nice?"

"Yeah, he's a good guy." His brows creased, and he laughed derisively. "He's also my—well, he used to be my brother-in-law."

Jacey's eyes widened with surprise, and Kale went on slowly, "He's really a good guy. I have nothing against him. He seems to have his head in the right place anyhow."

Jacey studied Kale closely, wondering if she should broach the subject. Then making up her mind, she asked, "Grant—he told me your wife was killed in an accident. I'm sorry."

Kale's jaw tensed slightly. "Yeah, it was four years ago."

He didn't elaborate as he drove through the city. Soon he pulled into the packed parking lot of a small Mexican restaurant. He shut the engine off, then leaned back against his seat.

He stared out toward the busy street and spoke quietly. "Adrian and I were married a little over six years when it happened. She was driving into Provo. The truck—it hit some black ice and threw her out of control. She crossed the median and hit a semi-truck head on."

"Kale," Jacey's eyes suddenly burned with emotion, "that's terrible."

Kale took a deep breath and shook his head. "She was heading into town for a doctor's appointment. She was—she was a little over four months pregnant with our daughter."

"Kale—no," Jacey whispered, her heart twisting. Memories of her own parent's accident flitted through her mind. Her grief and anguish had seemed unbearable at that time. She couldn't begin to imagine what Kale's grief would have been.

Kale turned to look at her. His eyes were haunted, but he gave her a small smile, then shook his head. "I should have been there with her that day. We'd had a bad snow storm come through, and it caused a lot of damage to the barn. I decided to stay behind to fix it. She wanted me to go, but I argued with her. I told her it needed to be fixed that day."

"Kale . . ." Tentatively she reached out to touch his hand.

He glanced at her, then pulled her hand into his and squeezed her fingers tightly before he went on, "Adrian and I spent nearly four years trying to have a family. At first she wasn't able to have children. The doctors told us she never would. Then one day, she was pregnant. It was the miracle we'd been praying for." Kale shook his head. "Everything seemed so perfect at the time, and then suddenly, she was gone, just like that. I think I was in shock for the first year. Her family—they took it hard. I should have been driving. I shouldn't have sent her on by herself. Her family blamed me for a long while after it happened. We all had a terrible time dealing with one another.

"We've just gotten on good terms with each other—within the last year or so, ever since Tom and Ally started seeing each other." Kale laughed and smiled. "I think it nearly knocked Adrian's parents for a loop when my sister and their son announced the engagement—but like I said, Tom's a good man. He'll make Allison happy."

"Kale that's awful—I don't mean about Allison and Tom, but—they blamed you?"

Kale nodded. "It was . . . hard for them. I blamed myself for a lot longer. It's been tough, but . . . well, I've come to terms with what happened. I sometimes wonder how things would have turned out if I hadn't stayed behind to fix that blasted barn, but— there's no sense in dwelling on it. She's gone. I can't bring her back or turn back the time. I loved her so much, but . . . I know she'd want me to move on and I'm trying. I've just been taking things one day at a time. Dad and Mom were—well, *are*—a huge support, and between work and the farm, I've survived."

Jacey met his eyes with a poignant smile. "Grant said you had started—" She stopped suddenly, shocked that she had been about to mention dating. She could feel herself turning red.

Kale smiled knowingly. "Dating?"

Jacey blushed openly, and Kale laughed.

"Well—he mentioned someone," she stammered.

"Cindy," Kale stated with a grin. "I think Dad and Mom think—or *hope* rather—that things are getting serious, but," he shook his head, "Cindy and I are only friends. I think Mom's tired of having two old, single children. I married late in life the first time. I was determined to finish my master's degree. Allison's done about the same. She wanted to finish up her degree. She's marrying later than a lot of other women around here, but—well, she couldn't be happier, and I'm happy for her and Tom."

He smiled lightly before he asked, "Hungry?" He nodded toward the small restaurant.

Jacey sighed and nodded. "Yes—and I love Mexican food."

"I know. I cheated. I asked Blaze yesterday," he admitted with a grin.

"You did cheat." She laughed.

Kale winked and stepped from the truck. As he opened her door to help her out, Jacey was amazed to notice that the rain had stopped and the sun was already beginning to break through the thinning clouds.

"That was a quick storm," she commented as they stepped inside.

• • •

Jacey eagerly dipped a warm, crisp tortilla chip into the bowl of green salsa. She smiled at the tangy hint of lime and nodded her approval. "It's great."

After swallowing his chip, Kale nodded. "So far I'm impressed. That's the best salsa I've had in a long while."

She laughed, then focused her attention on the menu. A moment later, the waitress returned and wrote down their orders.

The young girl left with a smile, saying, "I'll get it out as soon as I can."

"So how often do you travel for work?" Jacey asked once they were alone.

"Depends. I go once or twice a month, usually. Mostly I travel to Alaska, but I've been to the Middle East a couple of times."

"What do you do exactly?"

Kale smiled as he replied, "I spend a lot of time surveying the land and areas where they want to open new wells or close old ones. It usually depends on what the companies need at the time. So I dabble in a little bit of everything. I—" Kale paused as his cell phone rang. He glanced down and pulled the phone from his pocket. "Sorry." He glanced at Jacey again and then flipped the phone open. "Hey," he spoke into the phone.

Jacey reached for the bowl of tortilla chips and ate a few more as Kale took his phone call. She half listened to his one-sided conversation.

"Yeah," he commented gruffly, and Jacey glanced up. His forehead suddenly creased, and his eyes look worried. He glanced momentarily toward Jacey, then asked into the phone, "Did you check Mark's barn? Their cat just had kittens; he might have stopped there."

Jacey paused as she was about to bring another chip to her mouth. She held her breath and watched Kale carefully. Was he talking to Helen or Grant?

"Blaze?" she whispered. Kale nodded. "What is it?" she asked, sitting up straighter as her heartbeat quickened.

"Hold on, Mom." Kale pulled the phone away from his ear and spoke to Jacey. "They've just lost track of Blaze, that's all. Marcie called and asked if he could come by to play with Jason. I guess Mom told Blaze he needed to wait until we came back. Blaze was kind of upset, and he's wandered off somewhere."

Jacey grimaced and shook her head, frustrated. "How long has he been gone?"

"Only about fifteen minutes or so," he replied. Jacey bit down on her lower lip nervously, and Kale added, "He could have gone anywhere. Try not to worry. Mom says Dad is out checking the barn and sheds right now."

"He didn't try taking the horse by himself, did he?" Jacey questioned suddenly.

Kale placed the phone back against his ear. "Ocotillo's still around?"

He waited for a few short moments, then he nodded toward Jacey before he spoke to Helen. "Well, if he didn't take the horse, chances are he headed out toward Mark's place. More than likely he just got sidetracked. You might also want to send Dad to check out my place. He may have gone to see the colt."

Jacey exhaled noisily and she ran a hand across her forehead just as the waitress brought their steaming platters of food. The young waitress looked apologetic as she placed their plates in front of them. Jacey gave her a quick reassuring smile.

"Thank you," she told the girl quietly before she turned her attention back toward Kale.

"Okay—it's all right, Mother. He'll turn up," he reassured Helen calmly. "All right—I'll tell her. You too, bye."

Jacey's nerves jumped when Kale shut the phone with a sharp click.

"They still haven't found him. Apparently, Pops already checked my place, and Mark's out checking around his yard."

Jacey ducked her head and breathed deeply. "I can't believe he would just wander off like that. He was in a terrible mood this morning—oh, that kid. When I get home . . ."

"He hasn't been gone too long, Jacey. Try not to worry. Chances are he'll turn up at Mark's place. Do you want to go back?" he asked.

Jacey groaned and glanced down at her steaming plate of tamales. "That boy. He has such a terrible temper when he doesn't get his way. I can't believe he would do this."

"Has he wandered off before?"

Jacey nodded. "Once or twice. I'm sorry, but maybe we should go back."

Kale smiled understandingly and pushed away from the table. "I think we better."

Jacey glanced again at the plates of untouched food. "I'm sorry, Kale." She glanced at him apologetically, and Kale chuckled as he left a wad of cash on the table.

"I'll take a rain check." He smiled playfully.

FIFTEEN

Jacey stared unseeing out the truck's passenger-side window. She bit her lower lip. Where had Blaze disappeared to? It was true—he had run off in the past, but he had always come back sooner than this. Jacey knew that if he heard Grant or Helen calling him, he would have come. Where had he gone? She ducked her head and clasped her hands tightly together, trying to still their sudden trembling. She glanced toward Kale. His jaw looked tense, but he caught her eye and smiled. He reached out to hold her small hand in his.

"Hey, try not worry, darlin'," he told her calmly. "I'm sure they'll have found him by the time we get there."

He gave her hand a quick squeeze before he brought it up against his lips to place a feather-light kiss against her fingers. Jacey inhaled sharply as his hot breath brushed against her cool fingers. She could hardly believe the sudden turn her and Kale's relationship had taken.

"It'll be fine. He'll show up," Kale continued gently.

"I can't help worrying," she whispered, turning to watch the fields and houses rush by. "He would have come when he heard them yelling for him. I'm sure he would have, but he was in a horrible mood—I just don't know what to think."

Kale squeezed her hand but said nothing as he pressed on the gas pedal. Jacey felt the truck pick up speed. By the time Kale turned onto the dirt lane leading to the Jackman's home, Jacey's stomach was churning with raging nerves. Kale slowed momentarily as he passed the Grace's home. Mark and Marcie's yard was empty, and Mark's truck was gone.

"They're probably up at Mom and Dad's place," Kale commented as he pushed the truck toward the Jackman's farm.

The sound of gravel popping against the truck's large tires filled the air when Kale pulled into the driveway. Jacey caught her breath as Helen rushed out onto the porch. Without waiting for Kale, Jacey jumped from the vehicle and rushed toward the porch.

"Have you found him?" she asked.

The older woman wiped tears from her eyes and shook her head. Jacey wrapped her arms around her tightly.

"I'm so sorry," Helen wept. "Grant and I—we've been searching. But we can't—can't find him." She sniffed loudly.

Jacey shook her head, feeling frightened. "Where could he have gone?" she asked, turning to Kale as he came up behind her. He placed his hands firmly on her shoulders, and she met his troubled expression.

"Did Dad check my place?" he asked Helen.

Helen nodded somberly and sniffed again. "Mark's searching with him. They're checking up in the hills now. But I haven't heard from them yet." She choked back a sob. "I'm—I'm so sorry, dear." She turned agonized eyes toward Jacey.

"This is not your fault." Jacey hugged her.

Within moments, she heard the unmistakable sound of Grant's truck bumping down the lane from Kale's property. Jacey held her breath as the truck pulled into the yard. Grant jumped from the truck and moved with agitated steps toward them.

"That boy come back yet?" he called, and Jacey gripped Kale's forearm tightly.

Kale shook his head, and Helen began to sob in earnest.

"He wasn't in the hills?" Kale asked as Grant mounted the steps.

He eyed Jacey, shaking his head before he replied gruffly, "I'm so sorry about this, darling. Mark borrowed Athabasca's Gold. He's searching the fields. I've checked all the outer buildings.

I can't think where the boy could have disappeared to." Grant shook his head. He removed his worn hat and ran a hand through his thinning gray hair.

"Where could he have gone?" Jacey breathed.

Kale placed an arm around her shoulder and pressed a soft kiss against her temple. "We'll find him," he whispered. Then he spoke to Grant, "I'm going back to Mark's place to check the sheds and barn again. Did Marcie stay at the house?"

Grant nodded, and Kale pulled away from Jacey as the older man replied, "She's been sitting by the phone in case he showed up at their place. Jason's been out searching the barn and the loft. Last we heard, they hadn't seen him yet."

Jacey raised a hand to her throbbing head. "Maybe we should call the police. He wouldn't have stayed away for so long. He would have come by now."

Helen moaned, and Grant placed a thick arm around his wife's shoulders to squeeze her tightly. "It's all right, darling, but I think Melissa's right. We'd better call the station."

Jacey paled visibly. She squeezed her eyes shut, then jumped when her cell phone rang. Its shrill jingle sounded through the material of her purse, and she raced to answer it. If Blaze had gotten lost, if he had found a phone, he would be calling her. She hurriedly retrieved the ringing phone and answered it breathlessly. "Hello, Blaze?" she called into the receiver.

All eyes turned toward her, anxiously, and Jacey held her breath. "Hello?" she said again.

"Hello—*Melissa*." Jacey suddenly froze at the sound of John's all-too-familiar voice.

Her body grew rigid, and she breathed his name, "John."

Kale's eyes immediately met hers, and she felt him tense. Jacey moved numbly to sit on the top step.

"I suppose by now you're missing our son?" John laughed, and Jacey choked back a sudden sob.

"No—Blaze! Where is he? What have you done with him?" Jacey's blood ran cold, and her hands trembled violently.

"Jacey?" she heard Kale ask, and he moved toward her. She met his eyes as he knelt in front of her.

"John, give me back my son," Jacey spoke, taking courage in Kale's nearness.

John's mocking laughter seemed to swirl around her. "If you want to see our son again, then you listen close," he replied sternly. "I'm staying at a hotel in Payson. Do you know where Payson is, Jacey?"

"Yes," she whispered into the phone.

"It's the first motel on your right as you exit the freeway. I'm in number forty-three. You come and we'll talk. You come alone, Jacey. I don't want cops. And if you bring that new boyfriend of yours or anyone else, you'll never see my boy again. Do you understand?"

Jacey nodded and numbly replied, "Yes." Then she asked quietly, "Have you hurt him?"

John laughed. "No, but I suggest you do exactly what I say— honey."

Jacey shook her head and replied more firmly, "I want to talk to him, John." John laughed again, and Jacey gritted her teeth. "I want to talk to Blaze," she yelled into the phone.

"No," he replied icily. "Now do as you're told, Jacey. I'm not playing games."

The phone clicked deafeningly in her ear. Jacey shut her eyes, squeezing them tightly. She felt Kale's arms move around her waist, and she opened her eyes to meet his worried gaze.

"John has Blaze?" he asked.

Jacey nodded mutely.

His eyes hardened, and his jaw tensed visibly. "We'll get him back, Jacey," he spoke firmly, and Jacey shook her head, choking back a sob.

Grant and Helen moved closer before Grant voiced gruffly, "Who is John? And who in the Sam Hill is Jacey?" he asked, watching her and Kale closely.

Jacey stiffened, and Kale stood to face his parents.

"I'm Jacey," Jacey spoke quietly and weakly as she stood up next to Kale to face the older couple.

Helen's mouth fell open, and she glanced back and forth between Jacey and Kale. Grant shoved his hands into the back pocket of his worn coveralls and eyed Jacey closely.

"Please," Jacey entreated. "Please understand. I am so terribly sorry. My name is Jacey Grayson, and John—he's my ex-husband—I don't have time to explain right now." She turned to face Kale. "I have to go now. He has Blaze. I have to get my son."

Jacey cast an apologetic glance toward Grant and Helen and then moved past Kale to descend the porch stairs.

"No, Jacey." Kale stepped behind her, placing a hand on her shoulder. "You're not going alone. Where does he want you to meet him?"

Jacey shook her head, discouraged. "I have to meet him, Kale, and I have to do it alone."

"Not alone, Jacey," he replied tightly.

She swallowed and straightened her shoulders. "I have to go *now*," she turned, pulling from his grasp, and moved toward her Jetta.

Her hands were surprisingly steady as she inserted the key to unlock her door. Kale's boots crunched against the gravel as he followed. Again she felt his hands on her shoulder, and he turned her gently to meet his gaze.

"We'll call the police," he told her.

"No, Kale," she replied pleadingly. "Don't you understand? No police. I'll never see my son again. Please, Kale, let me go." Her voice trembled as she brushed off his hands and slid into her car.

Jacey heard Kale's frustrated grunt. She briefly caught a glimpse of him as he ran his hand through his hair in irritation and stepped away from her car. Not hesitating, Jacey started the vehicle and backed out of the driveway. She turned onto the rutted lane leading toward the main street. Her knuckles showed white as she drove her vehicle through town and turned onto the freeway entrance. Pressing the gas, she pushed the Jetta to ninety and headed toward Payson.

• • •

Jacey moved with determination as she stepped from her car and faced the slightly run-down motel John had spoken of on the phone. She took a deep calming breath and searched for room forty-three. Her steps sounded loudly as she hurried down the sidewalk that ran along the motel's length. Her ragged breathing echoed in her ears.

"John, it's me! Open the door," she called with a pounding knock once she located the correct room. She held her breath, listening for noise inside, then beat against the door more loudly. "I'm alone—open the door!"

The door cracked open, and John's sneering face appeared above the lock chain. Then the door shut, and Jacey heard the sound of the chain being slid away. The door opened once again. Without a glance toward John, Jacey stepped into the room. Her eyes immediately fell on her son, sitting on the far bed.

Catching sight of Jacey, Blaze bolted from the bed and ran toward her. She pushed past John and stepped further into the room. The sound of the door slamming shut echoed vaguely in her mind as Blaze fell into her arms.

"Mom," Blaze spoke against her shoulder, and she knelt to pull him closer. "I'm sorry. I wanted to see Jason's kitties, but Dad saw me walking there," he explained remorsefully.

"It's all right, baby. It's going to be fine." She held him tightly before she pulled back to meet Blaze's eyes. "Did he hurt you?"

Blaze shook his head, "No. Dad said I had to go with him. I'm sorry, Mom."

Jacey turned when John's mocking laughter reached her from across the room. She turned back toward Blaze and whispered quietly, "Go into the bathroom. Don't come out until your dad and I are done talking."

"No," John spoke loudly, "you stay where you are, Blaze."

Jacey turned to face John, and he marched toward her with glaring eyes. "What do want, John?" She lifted her chin.

He smirked disdainfully. "I want my son."

"You have no right to be here. Our custody order clearly states that you have no visitation rights. I can have you arrested, John." She faced him daringly.

John's face contorted angrily, and his eyes narrowed. "You little witch. How dare you take my son!" he growled.

Jacey stumbled when his fist suddenly slammed against the side of her head. She gasped, raising her arm to block his second blow.

"No, Dad!" she heard Blaze yelling. She backed against the door just as John grasped her shirt.

He clenched the material of her blouse tightly in one fist, pulling her face closer to his. Jacey's breathing was heavy, but she eyed him courageously.

"We're going for a little ride." His hot breath brushed across her throbbing cheek, and his face contorted dangerously as he spoke to Blaze. "Blaze, go get in the car, and if you try to run, I'll be forced to hurt your mother."

Blaze quietly sobbed as he moved toward the door. Their eyes met, and she could read the panic in her son's expression.

"We're not going anywhere with you, John." She spoke firmly just as Blaze opened the heavy door.

A stream of light spilled across the motel's shabby carpet, and Jacey squinted. John's hold tightened against Jacey's shirt. He watched with narrowed eyes as Blaze left the room and moved toward the car parked just out front.

"You'll get in the car or—I'll hurt you where it hurts the most," John spoke against her ear, and Jacey's eyes widened.

"You would hurt our son?" she whispered.

John let her go abruptly, then shoved her toward the door. "Get in the car—in the front seat," he demanded.

As Jacey slid into the passenger seat, she glanced briefly toward Blaze. Tears streamed down his young face, and he brushed at them with agitated hands.

"It's all right, babe," Jacey whispered as John slid into the driver's side and started the engine. "Buckle up," Jacey called back softly to Blaze, and she listened to the click of his belt before she did the same.

John pulled out of the parking lot onto the street, and Jacey stared mutely out the passenger-side window. She had to get Blaze away from John. No matter what happened, she knew she had to get her son away from him.

"Where are we going, Dad?" Blaze called uncertainly from the backseat.

John glanced briefly in his rearview mirror. He turned a corner once he met Payson's main street and headed north. "I told you—for a ride."

Jacey swallowed and watched out the window, discarding one idea after another. She didn't know what John intended, but deep down she knew he didn't intend for her to walk away. They drove in tense silence as John navigated the streets of Payson. Soon he turned east and pushed the car toward the hills. They passed several neighborhoods, and Jacey couldn't help but feel the sunny yards, with children playing happily, mocked their dire turmoil.

She took a deep breath, then asked into the silence, "How did you find us, John?"

John glanced at her and grinned cruelly. "You aren't that bright, Jacey. It was simple to track you to Detroit, and once that tramp you were living with saw me, she spilled everything."

Jacey paled. "Melissa—what did you do to her?"

He smiled maliciously. "I had an associate take care of it."

She shook her head, grasping the door for support. "You— you killed her," she whispered.

She heard Blaze's muffled whimpers coming from the back. *No!* Jacey's mind screamed, and her heart thumped painfully against her chest. *Melissa—what has he done?* She had to get Blaze away from John, but how?

As they drove away from the more populated neighborhoods of the small city, the road grew narrow. Thick oak shrub closed in on the car as John drove up a winding road. Soon, oak faded into taller cottonwoods, and then to towering pines as the car continued its climb higher along the twisting mountain road. They passed several vehicles, and Jacey watched with fearful eyes as John took the sharp bends at an alarming speed.

She held tightly to the car's door and asked, "Where are you taking us, John?"

His silence only confirmed what Jacey already knew. He was going to kill her. She inhaled several times before she whispered, "Promise me that Blaze will be all right."

John glanced at her out of the corner of his eye but remained silent.

"Promise me," she repeated more firmly.

She heard Blaze stir in the back seat of the car, and she glanced at him. His wide eyes met hers, and she forced a weak smile.

Tears filled his eyes, and his jaw clenched tightly. "Dad—" he began quietly, "please don't hurt Mom."

"Blaze," Jacey shook her head, "it'll be all right."

Blaze trembled visibly, and he sat up straighter in his seat. "Dad—I didn't tell anyone, I swear. Not a soul. You—you said you wouldn't hurt Mom if I didn't tell. I didn't tell, Dad—honest," he spoke quickly, and Jacey's eyes widened.

John glanced briefly in the rearview mirror but still didn't speak.

"What are you talking about, Blaze?" Jacey asked before she turned to John. "What is he talking about, John?" she pressed, her voice growing rigid with ever-increasing alarm.

John laughed malevolently and glanced toward Blaze. "Tell her, son." Blaze shook his head, and John's eyes narrowed. "Tell her!" he screamed. Jacey and Blaze jumped. John smiled sardonically, then repeated, "Tell her, Blaze."

Blaze's terrified expression fell on Jacey, and she breathed deeply before she asked, "What—what is it, babe?"

Blaze trembled, and Jacey reached back to grasp one of his cold hands in hers. She squeezed gently. "Please tell me, Blaze. What did your father do?"

"He—" Blaze began in a shuddering voice, "he shot—a lady and some guy. I was with him—he had me stay in the car," Blaze murmured weakly. Jacey's eyes widened in disbelief.

Blaze turned toward John, and his eyes overflowed with fat tears. "Dad—I didn't tell anyone, I swear. You promised you wouldn't hurt Mom." He began to sob in earnest, and Jacey turned horror-filled eyes toward her ex-husband.

"You *did* do it. . . . You killed that woman—and that reporter—with our nine-year-old child in the car?" She breathed incredulously. "How—how could you do it? He's only a child."

John sneered, and Jacey watched him, disbelieving. "He's old enough to become a man."

She shook her head. "You're crazy!"

Instantly John's fist slammed against the side of her face,

sending her head reeling toward the window. She gasped as her head hit the thick glass with a sickening thud.

"No!" Blaze screamed.

Jacey grasped her head. "I'm—I'm fine." Her voice trembled as she sat up, holding the side of her head. She could feel a painful knot forming against the side of her skull. "Blaze, hush," she soothed dazedly.

Blaze's sobs filled the car, and Jacey studied John carefully. His jaw clenched, and his knuckles tightened as he maneuvered the car around another sharp bend in the road. Her breathing sounded loudly in her ears, and she ducked her head to stare at her pale, trembling hands. *I can't let John kill me! What will happen to my son? John's a monster.* Jacey shut her eyes tightly. *Please, God in Heaven, wherever you are, please help me. Protect my child,* she begged. *Give me strength and courage. I can't let him take my baby.*

Jacey opened her eyes and took several calming breaths as she watched the mountain landscape rush by in a dizzying haze. Her head was throbbing, and she reached a tentative hand toward the swollen spot. Blaze's sobs had quieted. Unbuckling her seat belt, she turned in her seat to smile weakly.

"Momma," Blaze whispered, reaching for her hand.

She grasped his hand tightly, forcing her tears back. Then she turned her attention to John. His eyes stared straight ahead, and he slowed momentarily as they approached an especially tight turn in the road. *I have to stop him. I can't let him take us away from the main road*, Jacey thought frantically. She let go of Blaze's hand, then suddenly she threw her body against John's. Without thought, she immediately dug her nails into the side of his face.

John howled angrily as he fought for control of the car. He slammed on the brakes, and the car skidded to a staggering halt along the side of the highway. Jacey fought against him as he struggled to push her off. He shoved her away, and his fist slammed against the top of her head. Her neck twisted painfully, and she fell back, gasping for breath.

John's expression was livid as he pulled a gun from the inside of his coat and pointed it toward Jacey. Blaze's deafening screams filled the small car.

"Shut up!" John screamed.

Jacey glared as John moved the gun toward her head.

"Shut up! Now! I said shut up. Shut up!" John's face contorted in rage. "I'll kill her, right here and now!"

"Blaze," Jacey called, and Blaze's screams quieted to deep, gulping sobs. "Blaze, don't cry, baby." Jacey kept her eyes on John. Blood dripped down the harsh angles of his face where her fingernails had left half-moon-shaped gashes. His breathing was loud and ragged.

"No, Dad," Blaze moaned.

John's eyes flicked toward Blaze, and he slowly lowered his gun, placing it back inside its holster. Without a word, he pulled the car onto the highway and within a few moments, he turned onto a narrow dirt road, hidden among the trees. The car's low bottom scraped loudly against larger rocks, and the vehicle jarred and bumped as they drove in silence down the dusty road. Sunlight filtered through the thick wall of trees on either side of them and cast dappled shadows on the road ahead. Soon the narrow trees opened into a circular turnaround where the road ended. The car's tires skidded in the soft dirt as John braked. The vehicle came to halt, and he slammed it into park.

Jacey's blood ran cold, and a shiver went down the length of her spine. She heard Blaze's harsh breathing. "What are you going to do, Dad? Dad—" he pleaded with a trembling voice.

John turned to Jacey, and his eyes narrowed. "Get out." He spoke calmly, but his face twisted in rage. Jacey shook her head mutely as he repeated, "Jacey—get out."

"No, Dad, please," Blaze implored, and Jacey turned toward her son.

"It's fine, Blaze. I'll be okay," she whispered.

Blaze shook his head, his face a terrified mask.

John shifted in his seat and eyed Blaze. "Stay here, Blaze. Don't you dare move from this car." He snarled, then added, "Your mother and I—we're going for a little hike in the woods."

Jacey could feel the blood rush from her head. She felt suddenly weak.

She took a shuddering breath as Blaze begged his father, "Don't hurt Mom, Daddy—please."

Jacey reached for Blaze's hand. Bringing it to her mouth, she kissed it hard. "I love you, Blaze. Please—do what your dad says."

"Get out, Jacey," John warned. She turned numbly toward the door and stepped out into the cool mountain air.

She shivered instinctively as John came toward her. He indicated with a nod of his head that she should precede him. In a daze, Jacey stepped away from the vehicle. Tears of frustration suddenly spilled down her cheeks as she caught sight of her son's tear-stained face, pressed against the window.

"Momma." She heard his muffled sobs and she choked back a terrified moan. *Please save my son. Lord, please, spare my life*, she begged in agony.

The world seemed to move in slow motion as John pushed Jacey away from his vehicle and into the thick woods. Sounds became exaggerated, and Jacey winced as her foot snapped a twig. The noise seemed to resonate around her. She tried desperately not to give in to the overwhelming tide of fear that threatened to consume her, but a terrible sense of hopelessness was beginning to encroach on her mind.

"You—you know you won't get away with this, John," Jacey called back, trying to keep the vibrations of panic out of her weak voice.

"Just keep moving," John growled. Jacey gasped loudly when a rabbit suddenly darted out from the brush in front of her.

She paused for a moment, and John snarled, "This is far enough. Turn around."

Woodenly, she turned to face the man she had once loved. "John," she whispered his name. She shivered when a gust of wind brushed across her body. "Don't do this. Think of our son. Please. You won't get away with this," she entreated.

John shook his head and smirked as he reached deep inside his pocket. Pulling out a black tube, he screwed it onto the end of his pistol.

A silencer. Jacey's eyes widened in desperation.

"You don't have to do this, John." She glanced behind him, making certain Blaze had not followed. She turned her attention back toward him. "John, think about Blaze," she whispered.

He shook his head and laughed mirthlessly. "You dumb broad. Do you really think that a few days in the can is going to bother me? You had me put away. You ruined my reputation, babe. I spent eight years putting up with your foolishness. I gave you everything a woman could want, and how did you repay me? You took my son." He grunted loudly. " 'It doesn't have to be this way?' " He shook his head and laughed scornfully. "You always did have mud for brains."

"John, you have to think of Blaze! Think about what this will do to him. He's your son!" Jacey screamed.

John raised the gun, and Jacey backed up, her eyes widening, as John replied, "Blaze—he's my new made-man. You—you are nothing, Jacey. You never were. The kid's better off without you." His eyes narrowed dangerously.

"No," she whispered, closing her eyes. Suddenly something rustled in the nearby bushes. Her eyes flew open as John's attention turned toward his left. Without thought, Jacey rushed him. His attention turned immediately back to Jacey as she slammed her body against his. The gun went off. She pushed him to the ground, sinking her teeth into his calf muscle. He yelped in pain and grabbed a handful of her hair.

"John, no!" Jacey cried as tears of pain sprung to her eyes.

She flung her arms wildly as he pushed her back off him and slammed her body against the rocky ground.

"So now all of the sudden you've got guts, huh, Jacey? You think you've got guts?" he screamed above her. His hot breath brushed across her face. He spat angrily as he stood. Stretching his arm, he pointed the gun against her head and muttered cruelly, "Good-bye, Jacey."

No! She shut her eyes tightly just as a loud shot split the air. Her eyes flew open when she realized the shot had come from the nearby trees. John jumped as another shot bit into the dirt near his feet, kicking up a small cloud of dust. Jacey's eyes darted toward the trees.

John swore loudly. "What the—?"

A third shot zipped through the air, this time hitting John in the foot, and Jacey watched with amazement as her ex-husband screamed loudly and fell to the ground.

"Run, Jacey—get out of there!" She heard Kale's voice call through the trees.

She stumbled up from the ground, glancing quickly at John who was struggling to retrieve his gun, only inches away. *Kale*, she thought dazedly. She glanced toward the thick trees just as John's hand closed around the pistol. Her eyes widened, and she bolted away, running toward a large grove of pines.

Her heart clambered against her ribs, and a bullet whizzed past her head. She heard the soft thump as the bullet bit into the rough bark of a tree directly in front of her. Her legs felt wooden, and she forced them to keep moving as she ran through the trees.

Another shot zipped past, and she jumped behind the trunk of an especially large pine. *Kale's here*, she thought wildly. *Blaze!* Her breathing was ragged and harsh. *I have to get Blaze.* She continued to stay within the cover of trees as she made her way back toward the spot where they had left Blaze.

Her steps pounded against the dusty earth. As she came out of the woods, she saw John's car ahead, still parked in the clearing.

"Blaze!" she called, drawing nearer. The vehicle was empty. "Blaze?" she cried desperately. "Blaze!" Where was he? Where had he gone? She spun around, searching the trees that surrounded the little clearing. Her eyes widened when she caught sight of Grant rushing up the dirt road toward her.

"Grant?" she called as she ran to meet him. "Blaze. Where—?"

Grant's breathing was labored as he caught her by her shoulders, "He's—he's down the road, in my truck. Come on, girl," he wheezed, letting go of her shoulders. He grasped her elbow, spinning her around.

She shook her head. "No. Kale—John's got a gun. He—I have to go back," Jacey panted, but Grant shook his head.

"Kale's got a bigger gun—cops on their way," he choked out, shoving Jacey roughly ahead of him.

SIXTEEN

Jacey and Grant jogged down the road. Grant's breathing was heavy and labored as they neared his truck. Jacey's heart took courage at the sight of Helen huddled with Blaze in her arms, secured in Grant's pickup truck. Blaze caught sight of Jacey when they reached the truck, and he pushed out of Helen's arms.

"Mom!" he called while Helen struggled to keep him in the truck.

"Get in, girl," Grant spoke gruffly, jumping into the driver's seat.

Jacey moved in next to Helen, and Blaze fell into her lap as the truck growled to life. The large tires spun in the soft dirt when Grant slammed the truck into reverse. He flipped the truck around, then sped down the narrow lane, back toward the main highway.

"Blaze, Blaze." Jacey gathered Blaze against her. She pushed her face against his wet cheek. Helen's arms came around Jacey's trembling shoulders, and Jacey fell into her comforting embrace, still clutching Blaze tightly.

"Oh my, dear, I'm so glad you're all right," Helen murmured. Her voice trembled.

Jacey's eyes filled with tears as she spoke Kale's name. "He saved my life." She shook her head, squeezing Blaze against her. "Kale—he—" Tears made words difficult, and she glanced at

Helen apprehensively. Helen's eyes met hers, and Jacey knew they shared the same fear.

Helen nodded and weakly added, "He'll be all right. Heaven knows them boys will be safe. They have to be."

Jacey gasped when the truck jolted against an especially large pothole, but Grant slowed only when he reached the main highway. Slamming on the brakes, he pulled up next to Mark's blue Ford pickup, and Marcie jumped out of the vehicle to meet them.

"Go on—get out. You three wait here," Grant directed, giving Helen's cheek a hurried kiss.

"Please be careful. You just aren't as young as you used to be." Helen choked back a sob and embraced her husband briefly.

Jacey scooted from the truck, and Helen quickly followed. Sirens wailed in the distance as they moved over to stand next to Marcie. Jacey watched with trepidation when Grant's battered pickup disappeared up the lane.

"Mark—is he all right?" Marcie asked in a trembling voice, and Jacey turned toward her.

She shook her head helplessly. "I didn't see them, but Kale shot at John. Kale told me to run, but I didn't see them."

Marcie swallowed hard, and she reached out to grasp Jacey's hand in hers. "They'll be all right." She nodded. "They'll be all right. Mark and Kale have been hunting in these mountains since they were just kids."

The distant sirens grew louder, and soon two patrol cars skidded to a halt near them. Helen rushed to meet the officers when they stepped from their vehicle. "They're up there." She pointed up the lane. "We've got Melissa—I mean Jacey and Blaze, but the men went up there after him."

The patrolman waved at a third squad car coming toward them, and it raced up the lane without slowing. More sirens sounded in the distance, and Jacey watched with wide, fearful eyes as another police car came into view. It rushed past them up the lane. One of the officers came toward Jacey and asked her shortly, "You all right, ma'am?"

She nodded and felt Blaze stir next to her. He buried his face against her side. The officer's radio crackled loudly, and he stepped away to listen to the communication. Jacey watched him closely, trying to hear what was being said. What was happening up there? Where were Kale, Mark, and Grant?

She felt Helen step closer to her, and she met the older woman's tortured eyes. Tears ran silently down Helen's cheeks, and she reached out to hold Jacey's hand just as the patrolman stepped back toward the three women.

"Your menfolk are all right. The officers met them on their way down—apparently they had John Trent hog-tied in the back of their truck. They're on their way down now."

Relief washed in weak waves over Jacey. She fell, sobbing against Helen's plump shoulder. The two women held tightly to each other until Blaze began to squirm. Jacey pulled away and reached for Marcie. She hugged her and smiled gratefully at the two women.

"Thank you—thank you both," she cried, wrapping her arms around Blaze.

"Kale's okay?" Blaze asked weakly. Jacey smiled down into his young face and nodded mutely. Her throat felt tight with checked emotion as she placed a kiss upon his forehead. "Thank you, God in heaven," she whispered against his brow.

She turned her gaze back to Helen. "I'm so sorry, Aunt Helen." Jacey shook her head and glanced down toward Blaze. "I can't thank you enough—"

Helen squeezed Jacey's hand. "Kale explained some—no matter who you are—we still love you. I'm so glad you and Blaze are safe."

"How did you know where to find us? John kept checking to see if anyone was following—how did you know?"

Helen chuckled a little, then explained proudly, "That city husband of yours wasn't watching for three different vehicles."

Jacey's eyes narrowed questioningly, and Marcie hurried to explain, "Kale and Grant drove by our place, apparently right after you left. They both had their trucks. Kale told us to follow him. I was outside searching for Blaze, and Mark had just gotten back from checking the fields. When we couldn't find Blaze, I called my sister, so she was there to help keep an eye on our kids. Mark and I grabbed his truck and followed Grant and Kale to Payson. There aren't too many motels in Payson, so we all parked a ways away from where we saw your Jetta parked and we watched.

"Kale called on his cell phone, and we worked out a plan. When we saw that man pull out of the parking lot with you and Blaze in his car, Mark followed first. We just kind of watched each other. Mark turned off after a few minutes, and then Kale followed you. Mark and I would come up behind Grant, and then when Kale would turn off, Grant would follow. We kind of just kept switching places. Every time one of us turned off, the other took the lead. We kept in touch using our cell phones until we lost our signals, but somehow one of us always had you in view," she finished.

Jacey's eyes widened. "I can't believe it. That's amazing," she whispered.

"Blessed thinking is what I say," Helen jumped in. "We weren't sure what that man had in mind for you, but from the little bit Kale told us, we didn't think he was up to much good. When we saw him push you out of the motel, well, that's when we called the police. Apparently they already had the heads-up to watch for a John Trent, least that's what they told Grant. He's friends with the local dispatcher."

Jacey shook her head, amazed, and tears rushed in rivulets down her bruised, dusty cheeks. "Thank you. You saved my life."

They hugged one another tightly, then pulled away when they heard the unmistakable rattle of Grant's truck as it bounced down the narrow road. Jacey watched with bated breath as Grant's truck came into view, followed by two police cars. Grant pulled over and allowed the first patrol car to pass. It pulled behind the Graces' truck and parked while the second drove by slowly. John's scowling face met Jacey's gaze briefly, and Blaze buried his face against her leg so as to avoid his father's glaring eyes. She stiffened and watched, her face a stony mask, as the car moved past her and turned onto the highway.

Jacey shuddered as the car disappeared down the curving mountain road, then she turned wide eyes toward Kale as he stepped out of Grant's truck, followed by Mark.

"Mark!" Marcie yelled her husband's name, and Jacey watched with a pang of emotion as Mark gathered Marcie in his arms.

Helen rushed to meet Grant, and Jacey stepped hesitantly toward Kale. She spoke his name tentatively.

Blaze suddenly pulled away from Jacey and rushed toward Kale, throwing his skinny arms around Kale's long legs. Jacey heard Kale's gruff laughter as he bent to pull Blaze into a tight embrace.

"It's good to see you too, kid," he murmured against Blaze's hair.

Kale glanced at Jacey over the top of Blaze's head, and her eyes filled with tears when he smiled in her direction. She moved closer to where Kale stood. Blaze stepped away as Kale moved toward Jacey. He approached her in long, even strides, then pulled her into a crushing embrace. She pushed her face against his strong chest and wrapped her arms about his waist, relishing the comfort of his nearness.

"Kale, I was afraid. You're all right," she sobbed quietly.

She felt his lips brush her forehead before he buried a hand in her long hair and held her for several minutes. Her body trembled with pent-up emotion, and she clung to him tightly.

"Come here, boy," Grant moved closer, and Jacey pulled away from Kale, feeling self-conscious.

She watched as Grant pulled Blaze against him, and Blaze lifted his arms around Grant's thick neck. Jacey smiled when Helen immediately moved in next to Grant and placed her arms around Blaze's thin frame as well.

Jacey glanced back toward Kale. "You—you saved my life. You saved Blaze," she whispered. "Marcie told me—thank you, Kale. Thank you, all of you."

Kale pulled her close, placing his hands against her shoulders, and she met his distressed eyes. "He—" Kale shook his head and glanced away. His fingers pressed against her shoulders. "If—if he had—I could have killed him," he finished gruffly.

He reached up to tentatively touch the bruise forming against her cheek before he pulled her against him once again. His hands closed around the small of her back, and Jacey let her cheek rest against the soft fabric of his T-shirt. She closed her eyes, then jumped slightly when she heard a loud cough from behind her. Kale stiffened, and his arms dropped away from her as she turned to face the newcomer. The man smiled and flashed his badge.

"Ms. Grayson, I'm Special Agent Parker with the FBI. We've met before." He smiled broadly. "We've been looking for you. Sorry we didn't get here sooner."

Jacey's eyes widened, and she stepped away from Kale. "How did you—?"

"How did we know Trent would be in town? How did we know you were here?" he asked with a grin. Jacey nodded mutely. "We've been attempting to track you down since last week when you, well, disappeared."

Jacey winced, but the agent grinned as Grant, Helen, Mark, and Marcie moved in closer to listen. Jacey glanced toward Blaze, and she forced herself to give him a reassuring smile. Grant was holding her son's hand tightly in his, and Helen had her arm placed possessively around his shoulders.

"A few days ago, the Chicago field office received a tip from an agent who has gone deep undercover into the Vizcaino crime organization. The agent said that John Trent was attempting to find you and your son. Trent had you tracked to Melissa McCoy's home in Detroit; thankfully John Trent's contact just happened to be our inside guy. Once Trent tracked you there, he paid our insider to dispose of Ms. McCoy and her daughter."

Jacey heard Helen's sharp gasp, and Jacey nodded for him to go on, raising a trembling hand to her throat.

Agent Parker smiled and continued quickly, "Ms. McCoy and her daughter are fine. Our insider was able to get the McCoys to a secure location where he delivered them safely into the hands of Agent Ronald. Then our insider staged the hit."

"Oh, my," Helen gasped.

Jacey heard Kale stir behind her, and she glanced at him when his large hand closed around hers.

"That was when we learned of Trent's plan to follow you and your son here, to Utah. I immediately flew out, but I was given orders not to move in until danger became apparent—" Agent

Parker paused when Kale grunted derisively.

"Unfortunately," Agent Parker eyed Kale before his eyes fell back to Jacey's, "we didn't get our information in time, and we are sorry." Agent Parker's gaze traveled across the small group. "Luckily, Grant Jackman's call came through the Utah field office's dispatch, as well as the local dispatch."

Jacey glanced back toward Grant and smiled gratefully before she asked, "What's going to happen to John?"

"Right now he'll be kept in our custody until he can be extradited back to Chicago. We're going to need to bring all of you in for questioning," Agent Parker informed them. Then he turned as an officer approached.

"I think we're all done here, sir," the officer informed him.

Agent Parker grinned. "Excellent," he said and turned back toward the group.

"If you will all follow Officer Jimenez in your vehicles, he will escort you to the Provo field office." Agent Parker nodded.

Mark and Marcie glanced about uncertainly before they moved toward their truck.

"Ms. Grayson, if you'll follow me, I'll drive you and your son to the office where we'll meet with Agent Ronald," Agent Parker explained as he turned toward his unmarked vehicle.

"Jacey and Blaze can stay with me," Kale said loudly.

Agent Parker turned, a smile playing at the corners of his mouth, but he shook his head firmly. "No, I'm sorry, but Ms. Grayson and her son will need to be escorted by myself and an officer," Agent Parker replied.

Kale's eyes narrowed in frustration, and he glanced at Jacey.

"Thank you, Kale," she whispered. Then she turned to face Helen and Grant and smiled sadly. "Thank you."

Helen smiled with tear-swollen eyes, and Grant nodded, patting Blaze on the back.

"Come on, Blaze." Jacey reached a hand out toward her son and he came to her, taking her hand in his. She gave Kale one last smile. "I'll see you soon, I hope." Then she and Blaze followed Agent Parker to his waiting vehicle.

• • •

Jacey groaned wearily as she lifted Blaze's sleeping body into her arms and carried him out to the field office's waiting area. After several hours of grueling interrogations, she had finally been released from the small, stuffy office where they had questioned her and Blaze incessantly. She laid Blaze on the soft couch that sat against the office's west wall, then stepped back and sank into an oversized leather armchair across the room. She watched the rhythmic movement of Blaze's chest as he breathed deeply and evenly. He was so precious to her. She had come so close to losing him. The thought nearly stole her breath.

She exhaled noisily and sank back against the soft cushion, closing her eyes. She felt physically and emotionally drained. Agent Parker and Agent Ronald had told her that she and Blaze would both need to be present at all the hearings in John's trial to testify against him. Blaze had been a firsthand witness to the murders of Sharon Ivan and Gary Walbeck. Jacey had listened with a tormented heart as her frightened son had related the incident back to the FBI agents.

It pained her that he would have to stand and testify against his father. He was so young, and Jacey knew the burden would be a dreadful one for him to bear. After all, John was still Blaze's father, and Jacey knew that Blaze loved him for the father that he had been.

She sighed. When she heard the unmistakable sound of footsteps drawing near, her eyes popped open. She glanced up to see Kale moving into the room. He paused when he caught sight of her, and her heart ached. He looked tired, but he smiled openly.

"Jacey," he spoke her name quietly and glanced at Blaze's sleeping form. "Poor kid—he's probably worn clean out."

Jacey nodded. "He fell asleep about an hour ago. He could barely keep his eyes open."

Kale's eyes searched her face, and he commented, "You look ready to collapse yourself—you all right, darlin'?" He came toward her, and Jacey stood to meet him. He pulled her into a tight hug before he asked, "What did you find out?"

Jacey sighed, pulling out of his embrace. "Agent Ronald and Agent Parker are flying with Blaze and me back to Detroit in the morning. We need to go to the field office there for more questioning. John's trial will be in Chicago; Blaze and I will need to testify." She felt Kale stiffen, and she met his narrowed eyes.

"You're going to back to Detroit?" he asked warily.

Jacey nodded and glanced at him. "Yes."

His shook his head, raking a hand through his hair, "When will they let you come back?"

Jacey's heart picked up a beat, and she whispered, "I don't know if we will come back, Kale." He exhaled loudly, and Jacey hastened to explain, "I—we don't really belong here. I mean I came out here to escape John and—"

"Mom and Pops understand, Jacey," Kale jumped in.

"I know—but I don't belong here." Jacey let her eyes fall to the floor, and she heard Kale sigh.

"Jacey," he began softly. He stepped closer to lift her chin gently with his finger. "Jacey, you have to know—I care about you. It's only been a few days, but I know how I feel, surely—" he paused, and Jacey's heart clenched tightly as she met his tortured eyes.

"Kale," she spoke his name in a whisper, "I care about you too. You've—you've been such a support—such a good friend these last couple of days . . . I—"

"Friend?" Kale replied, discouraged.

"Please, Kale," Jacey went on quickly, "I care for you too, but—but I need to go back. Please try to understand. When I married John, I disappeared. I lost myself completely."

"Jacey," Kale breathed her name, and she met his eyes.

"Kale, I don't know who I am. I have to go back—I need to find my own strength, and I need to discover who I am. I have to take care of Blaze and learn to survive on my own. I need to create a life for us, and I need to do it to prove to myself that I can. Blaze—he's going to need counseling, and I intend to see a therapist too."

"But, Jacey—"

"No, Kale, please," she entreated, "please understand. I have to take control of my life and I can't do it here. I love you all, so much, but I need to go."

Her eyes filled with tears, and she brushed at them with agitated hands. She felt Kale's hand close around her shoulder, and she looked up at him imploringly. "Please understand."

Kale's eyes softened, but Jacey could read his pain and she sighed. His hand dropped from her shoulder, and he turned around. Rubbing his jaw, he turned to face her once again.

"I understand, Jacey. I do," he replied.

Jacey forced a small smile. "I'll never be able to thank you enough. I—"

"You don't need to thank me, Jacey. Just—" He paused to shove his hands into the back pocket of his dusty jeans. "Will you ever come back? Will I ever see you and Blaze?" His eyes looked haunted.

Jacey shook her head sadly and wiped a tear off her cheek. "I hope so. I want—"

"Then I'll wait, Jacey. If it means giving us a chance—even a small chance—I'll wait. Just—just don't forget me, all right?" Kale said.

She choked back a sudden sob, and Kale stepped toward her, placing his hands on both sides of her face. He squeezed gently, and Jacey replied, "I won't forget you, Kale."

Their eyes met in silent understanding. He rubbed her cheek before he slowly leaned in to place a kiss on her lips. He leaned in slightly, letting his kiss deepen for only a moment before he pulled back, wrapping his arms about her trembling body. Then he whispered her name and stepped away.

"Tell Blaze I said good-bye."

She nodded. "I will. He'll miss you. I—I'll miss you too, Kale."

Kale nodded brusquely. "I've got to go now. Take care of yourself, Jacey."

"I will," she whispered. "Good-bye, Kale."

He swallowed hard, then gave her a small smile. Jacey watched with tear-filled eyes as he walked from the room. With a little sob, she fell against the chair and buried her face in her hands. She ached to call him back, but instead she shook her head and stared up toward the ceiling. She didn't want to leave. She had never truly felt at home in any place until now.

She loved Helen and Grant as if they were family, and she knew, with an ever-sinking heart, that she loved Kale, but if she stayed, she would never know if she could stand on her own two feet. She needed to discover her true self, and Jacey knew that if she was to love Kale and allow him to love her, she would need to forgive herself first, and then John. She had to find her self-worth, or she would never be Kale's equal. She would always feel less than she was if she didn't get the help she so desperately needed. She wouldn't place that burden on Kale. Burying her face in her hands, she let the tears come.

SEVENTEEN

Jacey blew out a long breath and pulled her thin jacket more securely around her when another gust of icy wind brushed across her body. She shivered, then turned with a smile when Blaze called down to her.

"Bye, Mom," he said. Jacey smiled up at him as he waved down at her from their fourth-floor apartment in Chicago's riverfront district. "Bye, Mom. I love you," he called again.

Jacey laughed happily. "I love you too, Blaze. Be good for Megan," she called back with a grin.

Blaze shook his head with mock exaggeration. "I will! Jeez, Mom." Then he said, "Hey, your taxi's here."

He pointed up the street, and Jacey turned to watch as the bright yellow cab pulled onto their street and drove slowly toward her. She signaled the driver before she turned her attention back to Blaze.

"I'll see you in a few hours."

She waved as the taxi pulled up to the curb. Blaze returned her wave before ducking back inside. Smiling, Jacey scooted into the back seat of the cab.

She told the driver, "145 North La Salle Street, please." Then she sat back and watched the city go by. She clasped her hands tightly in her lap when she noticed they were trembling and took a deep breath. She would be testifying at John's final hearing. She felt nervous to testify again, but she was grateful that it would soon be over. Blaze had been required to testify at John's previous trial for the murder of Sharon Ivan, and it had been a difficult thing for him to do.

With financial help from a special program, Blaze had been in counseling since they had first come back to Chicago, and he seemed to be handling things much better than before. Jacey had seen a rather dramatic change in his temperament, and he was able to talk more freely about John and what had happened. She knew that he desperately missed Utah, though. He spoke often of Grant, Helen, and Kale, and they had all stayed in touch over the last four months. Even Jason and Marcie had emailed several times.

She was grateful that they were still in contact. After saying a brief good-bye to Grant and Helen, she and Blaze had flown to Detroit where they'd been rushed to the field office for more questioning. She had soon been allowed to see Melissa, and their reunion had been a tearful affair.

She and Blaze had spent three days with Melissa and Jenny while Jacey had searched the Internet for an apartment in Chicago. Melissa had begged her to stay, but Jacey had felt that she and Blaze would be more comfortable in a more familiar city. She and Blaze moved back to Chicago, and Jacey had soon secured a job as a full-time secretary at a nearby medical clinic.

Jacey sighed and gazed out the window. She felt stronger than she ever had before and proud of her accomplishments. She had also been seeing a counselor who specialized in therapy for battered and abused women. Over the last few months, she had learned a lot about her abilities and weaknesses. She had worked hard to change her pattern of behavior and her self-esteem, and she was seeing vast improvements in her daily life.

Jacey had made friends with several other women in her therapy group who had experienced similar situations, and she had found strength in their support and encouragement. Since they had been back in Chicago, she and Blaze had grown together, and she now faced their future with hope.

She took a deep breath when her taxi finally pulled up along the curb of the city's courthouse, and she smiled when she caught sight of Melissa standing near the entrance to the tall building. She paid the driver and stepped from the vehicle. A gust of cold November air brushed across her body, and she rushed up the sidewalk toward Melissa.

"Hey, girl!" Melissa came forward when she caught sight of Jacey, and they embraced affectionately.

"Hi, how was your flight out?" Jacey asked.

Melissa groaned and laughed, grasping Jacey by the shoulder. "This stretch gets longer every time. It's a good thing the federal government pays for these flights. I can't believe this is the last time we'll have to do this."

Jacey nodded, glancing toward the large double doors apprehensively. "I'll be glad to have this behind me," she admitted. "How's Jenny?"

Melissa shrugged. "She's growing like a weed. She'll be taller than Blaze soon."

Jacey chuckled as they walked toward the large doors. "Blaze wants to take a trip out there for Christmas vacation. I think he misses Jenny, but you know boys—he won't admit it."

Melissa laughed loudly as they stepped through the doors, and Jacey paused for a moment.

"Ready for this?" she asked, reaching for Melissa's hand.

Melissa grinned. "Anything that involves getting that jerk put away for longer—I'm always ready."

Jacey smiled and laughed quietly as people brushed past her and Melissa. She took a deep breath and nodded. "Let's get this over with."

Her heels clicked loudly on the marble floor as she and Melissa crossed the expansive lobby and walked toward the courtroom. Jacey took a deep breath when they neared the crowded entrance, and she slowed when she caught sight of Kale standing among the conglomeration of people.

"He's here." Jacey paused and placed a hand against Melissa's forearm.

"Who's here?" Melissa asked. Then she suddenly smiled. "Oh, I see."

As if sensing her presence, Kale suddenly looked up from

his conversation with a short, balding man. He caught her eye and smiled warmly, then waved as the group of people began moving into the courtroom. Caught in the shuffle, Kale waved one last time before he disappeared into the crowded room with the others. Jacey raised a hand to her fluttering stomach. She wondered if he still felt the same about her. They had talked on the phone several times since she and Blaze had moved back to Chicago, and not once had he pressed her to come back. Their conversations had been casual and friendly, but nothing more. Seeing him now, Jacey suddenly felt the crushing pressure of her feelings for him. Did he feel the same for her still?

Throughout the trial, Jacey caught Kale's watchful gaze on her a number of times, and she listened intently as Kale gave his testimony against John. This was the first trial in which Kale had been asked to testify. He was here representing the whole Jackman family. Helen, Grant, Marcie, and Mark had all given written testimonies, which were read during the trial. Jacey stiffened when John's hateful eyes fell on her during her own concise statement.

Soon the trial was over, and Jacey breathed a sigh of undiluted relief as the judge announced a guilty verdict against John. Melissa hugged her tightly and grinned sardonically at John as he was led, handcuffed, from the room. Jacey's tense body relaxed when the trial was adjourned and all participants were released.

"That monster's finally going to stay where he belongs," Melissa commented when they stepped back into the wide lobby. "I still can't believe what he put you through."

Jacey chuckled humorlessly. "I'm just glad it's over. Blaze has been through enough. Testifying against John wasn't easy. He even helped the police locate Gary Walbeck's body. John dumped him in a man hole. No child should ever experience that sort of horror."

"Oh, Jace," Melissa breathed. She reached out and grasped Jacey's hand. "It's over now. It's done."

Jacey nodded. A weak smile touched her lips. "It's done," she repeated.

When they reached the middle of the lobby, she turned and watched for Kale expectantly. Soon she caught sight of his dark head emerging from the cramped courtroom, and she watched with bated breath. He was talking with a tall blonde, and he smiled openly at the woman. Then catching sight of Jacey across the room, he hurriedly shook the woman's hand and turned toward Jacey. His steps were sure and steady as he crossed the crowded lobby, and Jacey couldn't help but smile when Melissa muttered quietly, "Wow, too bad he's my cousin."

She cast a quick, exasperated glance toward her friend, and Melissa laughed as Kale approached with a somewhat timid smile. "Jacey, how are you?" he inquired.

"Kale—it's good to see you," she replied with a soft smile.

"How's Blaze?" He shoved his hands into his coat pockets.

"Good. We've been staying busy. How are Helen and Grant?" she asked pleasantly, and Kale nodded again.

"They're doing well." He paused, then added, "You look great, Jacey."

Jacey felt a slight blush creep up her neck just as Kale's eyes darted toward Melissa. "Oh—Kale, this is Melissa, the *real* Melissa McCoy."

Jacey laughed and Kale grinned, extending his hand toward his cousin.

"Hi, Melissa. It's really good to finally meet you." He shook her hand. "The real you." He winked, and Melissa grimaced playfully.

"Yeah, about that—sorry." She laughed.

Kale grinned broadly and glanced meaningfully at Jacey. "I didn't mind the substitute."

Jacey blushed, bit down on her lower lip, and met his open gaze.

Melissa chuckled. "I think that's my cue to leave." She placed a hand on Jacey's forearm. "I'll leave you two to catch up." She hugged Jacey tightly and gave her a knowing smile. "I'm staying in town until tomorrow afternoon. Call me later, girl."

"I will. Thank you, Melissa. And take care."

"Will do, babe. See you." Melissa squeezed her hand and turned to Kale with a grin. "See you later, cousin."

Kale laughed. "I'll see you again when you come out this spring."

Melissa grinned. "I'm looking forward to it. Give Uncle Grant and Aunt Helen my love and tell them I'll give them a ring soon." Melissa winked and then walked away, leaving Jacey standing alone with Kale.

Jacey watched Kale carefully and then replied, "It's great that they'll all finally get a chance to meet."

Kale nodded. "Mom and Pops are looking forward to it."

"How are they? I haven't talked with them for a week or so."

"Good. They miss you, though. Ocotillo's missed Blaze."

Jacey laughed softly. "That boy—he drives me nuts over that horse. He brings the picture that Grant sent him of Ocotillo everywhere. That's all he talks about—going back to Utah and his horse. He made your arrowhead into a necklace. He loves to show it off at school."

Kale chuckled openly, and Jacey took a moment to remember how the corners of his eyes creased when he laughed. She had missed him.

"He's a good kid," Kale replied, and Jacey nodded her agreement. Kale suddenly took her hand. "Hey, my flight doesn't leave until this evening. Would you like to get some lunch?"

Jacey glanced at her watch and smiled. "Yes, but I told Blaze's babysitter that I'd be back around three."

Kale nodded thoughtfully. "Well, that gives us a little bit of time then. I saw a café a few blocks up the street. Or we could go someplace else, if you'd like."

Jacey shook her head. "The café would be great. That way we won't have to catch a cab."

• • •

As they sat drinking their hot chocolate at a table for two, Kale asked, "Tell me, what you have been up to lately? It's been a while since the last time we talked."

Jacey was thoughtful for a moment before she replied, "Mostly I've just been working. Blaze is doing a lot better in school, and he's joined the school's basketball team. He has his first game this week."

Kale smiled. "Really? That's great. I'm glad to hear it."

Jacey nodded and took a deep breath. "We—we're getting baptized next week." Kale sat up straighter. "Blaze and I have been taking the missionary lessons over the past few weeks, and our baptism is scheduled for next Thursday."

"Jacey, that's wonderful!" Kale reached across to take her hand.

She smiled. "Blaze spent an afternoon over at a friend's house a few weeks ago, and when he came home he brought these two Mormon missionaries with him." Jacey laughed, remembering. "I couldn't believe that he would bring them home with him. He met them on the street, and when he discovered they were Mormons from Utah—well, he was so excited. They gave us the first lesson that afternoon."

Kale's eyes shone excitedly. "I couldn't happier for you, Jacey."

"I thought we'd call Grant and Helen tomorrow or the next day. I wanted to tell you first. I thought you might be at this trial."

"They'll be very happy, and I'm glad you told me."

"Blaze is ecstatic and I'm happy. Your church made quite an impression on us," Jacey admitted with a little laugh.

"I'd like to be there, Jacey, for your baptism. Is that all right with you? I'll fly back out," Kale replied earnestly.

Jacey felt her heart jump happily. "I'd really like that, Kale. The missionaries are going to baptize us. We've been going to church with them. The church house is only a few miles from our apartment, and the bishop lives just a couple blocks away. We love the other members. They've been so kind to both Blaze and me, and Blaze has made a lot of new friends."

"That's fantastic," Kale replied with a broad smile.

"So, how is everything back there? How have you been?" she asked quietly. Suddenly she wondered if he was dating Cindy what's-her-name again, and she held her breath uncertainly.

"Good, really. I've had those few trips out to Alaska that I told you about. The farm's doing well. Dad finished the plowing last month, and the animals are doing fine. We're just getting ready for winter now. We haven't had any snow so far."

The waitress brought their plates of food, and Kale smiled appreciatively as she set their platters in front of them.

Jacey nodded thoughtfully and sipped her cocoa. Silence stretched between them. She heard Kale sigh, then he spoke her name tentatively. "Jacey—"

"I've missed you, Kale," she cut in suddenly. Jacey raised her eyes to meet his.

His eyes broadened. "I've missed you too," he replied with a grin.

Jacey let her eyes drop to her plate of food. Her stomach turned with a sudden flurry of butterflies.

"Jacey—darlin', I can hardly do this anymore."

Jacey glanced up, and her eyes widened apprehensively as he went on.

"I know I said I'd wait, and I will wait if you need more time, but dang it, Jacey, I—" He paused and exhaled noisily. "Jacey, I'm in love with you. I think you know that. I loved you that very first day when I saw you standing in that barn. You can't imagine my shock when I saw you. You looked so beautiful, I could hardly mutter a coherent sentence, and it made me so angry. I knew you weren't who you said you were and—well, half the time I wanted to strangle you—but every time I looked into your eyes or saw you laugh or smile—honey, I wanted to strangle you and kiss you all at the same time. And then, those last few days together—" He stopped and shook his head, sighing loudly.

Jacey raised a trembling hand to her throat. "Kale," she whispered his name.

His tortured eyes met hers, and he groaned quietly, "Come home, Jacey. Give us a chance. You and Blaze—I love you both. I ache for you and—and I long to be a family. I know you were only there a while, but a few days was all it took for me to realize how I felt about you." He raked a hand through his hair and smiled tentatively. "I'm sorry, Jacey. I know this is too sudden, but—every time I talk to you over the phone, and now, seeing you here—I'll give you more time, honey. I didn't mean to spring this on you," he finished brusquely.

Jacey's eyes widened with emotion, and her voice trembled as she replied, "I've been so afraid you wouldn't wait for me. I love you, Kale."

He looked up, his expression tormented. "But you need more time?"

Jacey glanced down. Her mouth twisted thoughtfully, then she shook her head slowly, "No—no, I don't. I do love you, Kale. Blaze loves you . . ." She paused and Kale eyed her with a crooked smile.

"But?" he questioned. His eyes sparkled.

Jacey laughed suddenly as her nervousness gave way to delight. "But nothing, I want to come home, Kale. Utah *is* home. Just the few days that we were there, I truly felt at home. *You* are home," Jacey admitted. Kale grinned. "I feel stronger now, more than I ever have before. John—I let his abuse influence what I believed about myself. I believed I was weak, less than he was—"

"Jacey, honey, I would never—" Kale cut in, but Jacey shook her head slightly.

"I know, Kale, but I—please know that I don't want to be taken care of and coddled. I don't want pity. Grant once told me that every man needs a good partner. Kale, that's what I want. I don't just want to be your wife. I want to stay home and raise a family, but I also want to be your partner. I want to stand next to you—not below you or above you. I never want to feel less than I am again."

Kale smiled gently and his eyes shone with emotion, "Jacey—you will never be less. In our church, we believe that a man and a woman can be sealed together for time and eternity. Not just as husband and wife, but as helpmates for one another. I've always believed in that, Jacey. I've watched my parents all my life. Things haven't always been easy—things weren't always easy for Adrian and me—but I know that when we face things together, they always have a way of turning out for the best.

"I can't promise that things will always run smoothly, but I can promise you that I will never raise a hand in force against you, and I will never intentionally demean you. I love you, and you will never be less. Together, we will only grow." He squeezed her hand tightly. "You have strength, Jacey, more than you realize. It was that quiet strength that I fell in love with. No matter what, we can get through the tough times—together." He grinned. "And just as you say, as partners."

Jacey smiled, bringing his hand against her cheek. "I want that," she whispered.

"So do I." Kale's eyes narrowed, and he whispered gruffly, "I love you, Jacey Grayson. After you're baptized, you'll learn more about the temple. We can be sealed together as an eternal family—when it's time and whenever you feel that you're ready."

"Yes," she replied, laughing happily, and Kale's laughter joined hers. "Maybe," Jacey sighed blissfully, "maybe we should go tell Blaze?"

Kale nodded and slapped some money onto the table. The dishes clinked when he pushed away from the little table, and he laughed. "One day you and I will finish lunch together, but not today. Let's go get Blaze!"

Jacey smiled, and her eyes met his, amazed. "We can tell him," she paused, then laughed, "that we're going home—and he can finally see his horse."

BOOK CLUB QUESTIONS

1. Overall, how did you experience this book? What emotions did you experience while reading?

2. What motivates Jacey's actions? Do you think those actions are justified or ethical?

3. Jacey is frustrated and worried about the changes in her son, Blaze. Faced with her dilemma, how would you handle the situation?

4. Which characters do you admire? What are their primary characteristics and what did they bring to the story?

5. Did Jacey grow and change during the novel? If so, in what ways?

6. Can you pick out a passage that strikes you as particularly interesting or profound?

7. How did the different viewpoints enhance the story? For example, did you find John's point of view relevant?

8. Uncle Grant quotes, "It is better to lose your pride with someone you love than to lose that someone you love with your useless pride." Who is he referring to, and how could this quote be applied to your life?

9. Domestic violence is a central theme in this book. Throughout the story, people ask Jacey why she stayed with John so long. Why do you believe she stayed? Do you believe that society offers enough resources to help women in abusive situations?

ABOUT THE
AUTHOR

Mandi Slack was born in Price, Utah, and grew up in Orangeville, Utah, where she developed a great love of the outdoors. She enjoyed adventure novels as a child and has always been fascinated by books and writing. Mandi attended Utah State University, where she completed a four-year degree in special education. She currently resides in Santaquin, Utah, with her husband and family. In her free time, she enjoys camping, hiking, and rockhounding with her children.